THE SCIENCE OF
WEATHER
AND
CLIMATE

RAIN, SLEET, AND THE RISING TIDE

JULIE DANNEBERG

Illustrated by Michelle Simpson

Nomad Press

A division of Nomad Communications

10 9 8 7 6 5 4 3 2 1

This book was manufactured by Versa Press, East Peoria, Illinois
January 2020, Job #J19-10192
ISBN Softcover: 978-1-61930-850-3
ISBN Hardcover: 978-1-61930-847-3

Educational Consultant, Marla Conn

Questions regarding the ordering of this book should be addressed to
Nomad Press
2456 Christian St., White River Junction, VT 05001
www.nomadpress.net

Printed in the United States.

Titles in the Inquire & Investigate
Earth Science set

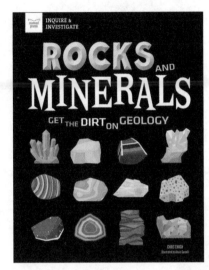

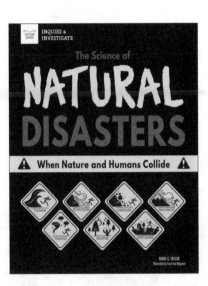

Interested in primary sources?

Look for this icon.

You can use a smartphone or tablet app to scan the QR codes and explore more! Cover up neighboring QR codes to make sure you're scanning the right one. You can find a list of URLs on the Resources page.

If the QR code doesn't work, try searching the internet with the Keyword Prompts to find other helpful sources.

🔍 weather and climate

What are source notes?

In this book, you'll find small numbers at the end of some paragraphs. These numbers indicate that you can find source notes for that section in the back of the book. Source notes tell readers where the writer got their information. This might be a news article, a book, or another kind of media. Source notes are a way to know that what you are reading is information that other people have verified. They can also lead you to more places where you can explore a topic that you're curious about!

Contents

Glossary ▾ **Metric Conversions** ▾ **Resources** ▾ **Index**

TIMELINE

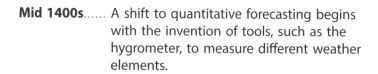

Mid 1400s...... A shift to quantitative forecasting begins with the invention of tools, such as the hygrometer, to measure different weather elements.

1450.............. Leon Batista invents the anemometer to measure wind.

1593.............. Galileo Galilei invents the first crude thermometer to measure temperature.

1643.............. Evangelista Torricelli invents the first barometer, known as Torricelli's Tube, to measure air pressure.

1776.............. Thomas Jefferson, along with other scientifically minded people of the time, makes daily weather observations for many years, including on July 4, 1776.

1870.............. The U.S. Weather Bureau is formed under the War Department.

1895.............. *International Cloud Atlas* is published, which provides a shared vocabulary and system for identifying clouds.

1920.............. The radiosonde, a box with weather instruments and a radio transmitter, is invented.

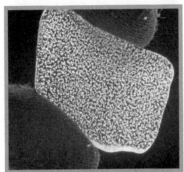

1936.............. The world's first televised weather forecast, complete with weather maps, takes place in England.

1950.............. John Von Neuman uses the newly created ENIAC (Electronic Numerical Integrator and Computer), the world's first general-purpose computer, to come up with the first computer-generated numerical weather predictions.

1960.............. The Television and Infrared Observation Satellite (TIROS 1) becomes the first satellite launched into space, allowing us to see what weather looks like from outer space.

1966.............. The U.S. National Meteor Center develops a comprehensive model of atmosphere.

1979.............. The Geostationary Operational Environmental Satellite (GOES) system is launched into orbit by NASA.

1982.............. The Weather Channel debuts on 24-hour cable network.

2011.............. The National Oceanic and Atmospheric Administration (NOAA) and the meteorological community launches talks about how to build a weather-ready nation.

2018.............. The *Parker Solar Probe* is launched to study the sun.

weather climate cirrus coral reef meteorology thermosphere troposphere front freezing rain climate change geothermal global warming supercell

ozone layer atmosphere radiosonde glacier vacuum ridge

climate eye cloud thermohaline exosphere blizzard hail water cycle current El Niño

nimbus sastrugi polar air mass fog axis eye wall mesosphere barometer paleoclimatology climatology organic aurora borealis wind shear NASA buoy trough

saturated Ferrel cell drought tropical fossil fuels offshore breeze strife arid stratosphere conservation cumulus anvil lightning proxy data methane humidity fluctuate cirrus disperse turbine equator conductive finite shock wave

continental air mass Arctic air mass iceberg global ocean currents barometric pressure friction

updraft evaporate circulate prevailing wind efficient stratus

hurricane Hadley cell precipitation Isobar emissions tornado

Doppler radar drone latent heat water vapor local winds variation forecast lattice NOAA

velocity stationary stable air average

nitrogen temperate dew point variable graupel

condense reservoir anticyclone core sample trade winds energy relative humidity transpiration habitat

atom evolve downdraft thunderstorm orographic cloud dropsonde accretion mist jet stream low pressure downslope wind upslope wind redistribute latitude leeward sediment water cycle radar experiential correlation satellite gradient molecule wind chill sediment current biomass predictable eye wall typhoon frost sleet storm surge tropical

Introduction ▶
What's the Weather?

WEATHER AND CLIMATE HAVE A UNIVERSAL EFFECT ON US ALL.

Why should you study weather and climate?

Weather and climate shape your everyday life and could very well shape your future. Understanding how your world works helps you to appreciate it more, as well as to protect it better.

The weather and the climate where you live controls your life in many ways. The daily weather might determine what clothes you wear, whether or not you go outside for lunch, and what activity you do after school. The climate of your area likely influences what kind of car your parents drive, what kind of house you live in, and, believe it or not, what food you eat and even what diseases you might get!

Although weather and climate have wide-ranging effects on our lives, many people do not truly understand the difference between weather and climate. Weather describes the daily variations of temperature, precipitation, wind, and cloudiness that are happening in your immediate world. Climate, on the other hand, is the average of those weather happenings during a long period of time.

Although weather changes from hour to hour and day to day, if we look at weather in a specific place for an extended period, we can detect patterns. Those patterns make up the climate of that area.

What are the predictable patterns in your area? Does spring usually start around the end of April or do you see trees blooming and grass turning green at the end of March? Do you get a lot of snow during the winter months or do the temperatures rarely dip below 70 degrees? When you answer questions such as these, you are describing the climate of the area in which you live. When you describe what is going on outside your window at this very moment, you are describing the weather.

> J. Marshall Shepherd, a past president of the American Meteorological Society, describes the difference between these two concepts this way: "Climate is your personality; weather is your mood."

VOCAB LAB

There is a lot of new vocabulary in this book. Turn to the glossary in the back when you come to a word you don't understand. Practice your new vocabulary in the VOCAB LAB activities in each chapter.

Do you have tornadoes where you live? This photo was taken in 1973 and it's one example of extreme weather!

Credit: NOAA Photo Library, NOAA Central Library; OAR/ERL/National Severe Storms Laboratory (NSSL)

ANCIENT TIMES

In ancient times, weather was unpredictable. Ancient people didn't have any tools to tell them when it might rain or snow or how long a drought would last. The earliest humans' quality of life was inextricably tied to the weather. The amount of food available to hunters and gatherers depended directly on rainfall and drought. Cold spells and heat waves weren't just uncomfortable, they could be deadly.

Ancient people made observations about the world around them and tried to control the weather by building temples, conducting religious ceremonies, and following cultural beliefs that grew out of the idea that the gods controlled the weather. As time passed, humans' ability to predict the weather often grew out of careful observation of nature.

PRIMARY SOURCES

(PS)

Primary sources come from people who were eyewitnesses to events. They might write about the event, take pictures, post short messages to social media or blogs, or record the event for radio or video. The photographs in this book are primary sources, taken at the time of the event. Paintings of events are usually not primary sources, since they were often painted long after the event took place. What other primary sources can you find? Why are primary sources important? Do you learn differently from primary sources than from secondary sources, which come from people who did not directly experience the event?

The temple of Poseidon in ancient Greece was built to honor Poseidon, the god of the seas.

credit: Ken Russell Salvador (CC BY 2.0)

Have you ever heard the saying, "Red sky at night, sailors delight. Red sky in morning, sailors take warning?" Sayings and folk wisdom sprang from a close association with nature and were passed down from generation to generation, in order to help people anticipate the weather.

Now, those sayings and bits of folk wisdom can be analyzed with our vastly improved understanding of how weather is created. We see that they were often based on real weather principles.

WEATHER TODAY

As time passed and our grasp of science grew, many great minds applied their thinking to growing a fact-based knowledge of weather. Today, scientists' weather knowledge is based on more and more sophisticated technologies and methods for gathering those facts.

> Radar and rocket ships, satellites and storm-chasing jets are just a few ways that we now have to learn about weather.

The National Oceanic and Atmospheric Administration (NOAA) is a government agency that uses cutting-edge technology and research to study climate and predict weather. This is important not just so that you know what clothes to wear tomorrow, but because understanding the weather and climate is a way to keep people safe and protect the environment.

According to NOAA, "Each year, the United States averages some 10,000 thunderstorms, 5,000 floods, 1,300 tornadoes and 2 Atlantic hurricanes, as well as widespread droughts and wildfires."[1]

How is a man walking a dog similar to the variability of daily weather versus the long-term trends of climate? Take a look at this short video to find out!

 dog walking weather climate

WEATHER WORDS

The more you learn about weather, the more you see words sprinkled throughout our language connecting weather conditions to emotion or life conditions. It is another subtle way that shows what an impact weather has on every aspect of our lives. For instance, when you are experiencing "brain fog," you aren't seeing things very clearly, just as in real fog. A relationship filled with strife and disagreement might be described as a "stormy" relationship. Can you think of any other weather words that describe emotions?

SCIENTIFIC METHOD

The scientific method is the process scientists use to ask questions and find answers. Keep a science journal to record your methods and observations during all the activities in this book. You can use a scientific method worksheet to keep your ideas and observations organized.

Question: What are we trying to find out? What problem are we trying to solve?

Research: What is already known about this topic?

Hypothesis: What do we think the answer will be?

Equipment: What supplies are we using?

Method: What procedure are we following?

Results: What happened and why?

NOAA also notes that, "About one-third of the U.S. economy—some $3 trillion—is sensitive to weather and climate." Understanding weather and climate is an important part of keeping businesses around the world thriving while maintaining a healthy planet.

What about extreme weather events? Flooding. Drought. Devastating hurricanes. Dust storms covering whole cities. Meteorologists and climatologists study these extreme weather events, not only to protect people today, but to help us understand them in order to protect our world in the future.

How much do you really know about what causes various types of weather?

Do you know what causes fog? Hail? Sunny summer days? When the weather forecaster on TV says that there is stationary low front, do you know what that means? What about climate change? Do you know what's causing it and how you can help prevent it?

In this book, you will learn the answer to these questions and more. You will learn about what causes wind and rain, clear skies and fluffy clouds. You will learn about global water and air currents that work like efficient conveyor belts constantly circulating to keep the earth's temperatures in balance. And you will see how it all fits together to create climates and how these climates are being altered by human behavior.

Understanding weather and climate is a complex undertaking. There are many interrelated factors at play, with one affecting the other, which in turn affects another. Weather is determined not only by what is happening in the sky, but also by what is happening on the ground and in the ocean.

An artist's rendition of the GOES-R weather satellite, 2012

credit: NOAA/NESDIS

As you learn about weather and climate, you begin to see how interconnected these different elements are, and how changes in one part of the world can affect weather and climate in another.

So, let's get started. Weather and climate—it's all around you. It follows you wherever you go. It's time to learn about it.

KEY QUESTIONS

- **Why is it important to understand the difference between weather and climate?**
- **How might ancient people have kept track of weather patterns without the modern tools we have today?**

For many years, the *Farmers' Almanac* was the source that people turned to, not only for farming advice and recipes, but also for weather predictions. While these weather predictions were not skillful, *The Old Farmer's Almanac* is a wonderful resource to find some old-time wisdom.

 weather sayings and their meanings

Inquire & Investigate

VOCAB LAB

Write down what you think each word means. What root words can you find to help you? What does the context of the word tell you?

climate, **drought**, **interrelated**, **meteorologist**, **technology**, and **weather**.

Compare your definitions with those of your friends or classmates. Did you all come up with the same meanings? Turn to the text and glossary if you need help.

To investigate more, try using other materials, such as rocks, leafy plants, glass, brick, and dark vs. light surface materials. What are some of your observations?

FEELING UNEVEN?

Different surfaces absorb the sun's heat at different rates. Think about oceans, rivers, lakes, beaches, cement parking lots, and newly plowed fields. Is there a difference between the amounts of heat absorbed by these different surfaces? What are the implications of those differences?

- **In your science journal, create two charts.** One chart will show the time and the temperature for each surface when in the sunlight. The other chart will show the same out of the sunlight.

- **Fill one container with the sand and an identical container with the same amount of water.** Place a thermometer in each container about an inch below the surface. You may need to tape the thermometers in place. Let the containers sit in the same spot in the room until they reach the same temperature.

- **Put the containers out in direct sunlight or, if possible, under heat lamps.** Check and chart their temperatures every minute for 15 minutes. Then, bring them back inside, out of direct light. Continue to record temperatures for 15 minutes.

- **Plot your data on a chart.** Is there really that much of a temperature difference between the types of surface materials? Why or why not? Did the two surfaces cool at different rates? If so, why might that be important?

Chapter 1 ▶
The Foundation of Weather and Climate

EARTH'S WEATHER BEGINS WITH THE SUN!

What are the basic ingredients of weather?

To truly understand weather and what causes it, you need to understand some of the basic ingredients required to make it. Those ingredients are the sun and the uneven heating of the earth's atmosphere.

Of all the planets in the solar system, why is Earth the one on which we live? Why isn't Earth red and dusty like Mars or broiling hot like Venus? The answer has a lot to do with what can be found in our atmosphere.

All the planets in our solar system rotate around the sun. They all receive its heat and light, and they are all surrounded by an atmosphere made up of a mix of gases. The earth, however is the only planet in our solar system that supports life.

Because of this, scientists sometimes refer to Earth as the "Goldilocks Planet," and for good reason!

In the fairy tale "Goldilocks and the Three Bears," Goldilocks lets herself into the bears' cottage when they aren't there. Hungry, she tastes the three bowls of porridge on the table before gobbling up the one that is just the right temperature.

Her pickiness continues as she investigates the bears' chairs and beds. She is always looking for the one that is "just right."

THE GOLDILOCKS PLANET

Lucky for us, even though it didn't start out that way 4.5 billion years ago, the earth evolved into a planet that was just right for many different forms of life. Here's why. For one, the earth is the "just right" distance from the sun. If we were closer to the sun, as are Mercury and Venus, our planet would be too hot. And if we were farther away from the sun, as is Uranus, our planet would be too cold to support life.

The earth is your home turf. How much do you know about this amazing place? Let the National Aeronautics and Space Administration (NASA) help you get acquainted at this website.

 NASA earth overview

A digital collage of the solar system that is not drawn to scale

credit: NASA/JPL

THE *PARKER SOLAR PROBE*

On August 12, 2018, NASA launched the *Parker Solar Probe* on a seven-year mission to learn more about the sun. Flying closer to the sun than any spacecraft has before, the probe will reach speeds of 430,000 miles per hour. It will use Venus to perform a gravity assist. This means it will take advantage of Venus's gravity to swing closer to the sun. Actually, it will do this several times as it gets closer and closer to the burning ball of gases! The plan is for the probe to get 3.83 million miles away—which sounds far away, but is much, much closer than any other spacecraft has come to the sun.[1]

Our "just right" placement in the solar system is helped by our atmosphere's makeup of just the right mixture of gases. These let in the perfect amount of the sun's radiation and helps to keep in the heat so the planet's temperature is balanced. Finally, Earth has just the right amount of water, without which life would not be possible.

If it weren't for the atmosphere, our distance from the sun, and our water supply, Earth would not have been able to evolve to the point where it could support human life. And the fact that it did is "just right" with us. Wouldn't you agree?

Let's take a closer look at all of the things that make our planet habitable.

THE SUN

All of Earth's weather begins with heat from the sun. On a summer afternoon, in most places around the globe, it's easy to make the connection between the sun and the temperature. What might be less easy to see are the links between the sun and rain showers, blizzards, tornadoes, and even hurricanes! But the relationships are there. Without the sun, none of those things would exist.

Before it generates weather, though, the sun must generate heat and then transfer it to Earth. But how?

The sun isn't made of rock but, like all stars, is a massive boiling ball of helium and hydrogen.

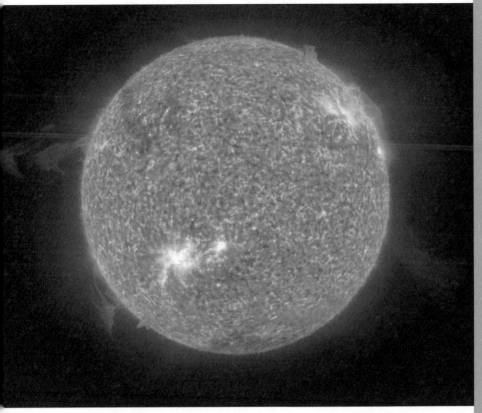

The sun

Credit: NASA/GSFC/SOHO)

Through a process called nuclear fusion, the hydrogen is constantly being turned into helium. This process creates enormous amounts of energy in the form of electromagnetic radiation, which then spreads out into space.

A very small portion of that energy travels the 93 million miles to Earth at the speed of light (186,282 miles per second), making it here in just eight minutes. Once the sun's energy hits the earth's atmosphere, much of it is reflected into space or absorbed by the atmosphere. Less than half of it reaches the land and oceans on the earth's surface.

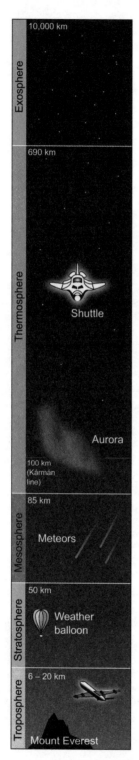

The energy that does reach Earth plays a crucial role in the presence of life on Earth, as well as controlling the planet's weather. Too much of the sun's energy getting in, however, could be disastrous for the planet. This is why the earth's atmosphere is so important.

THE ATMOSPHERE

Just as we need the sun to sustain life on Earth, we also need the atmosphere. This blanket of air separates our planet from the cold, dark vacuum that is outer space. It also provides us with oxygen to breath, serves as a shield to protect us from the sun's most harmful ultraviolet (UV) rays, and helps to regulate the earth's temperature by keeping heat from escaping.

The earth's atmosphere, held in place by gravity, consists of five layers. These layers serve different functions and are made up of different mixes of gases. Let's take a look.

The troposphere is the layer of atmosphere closest to the earth—this is where all life exists and where most of our weather takes place. The troposphere is about 10 miles deep at the equator and about six miles deep at the North and South Poles. Containing 90 percent of the atmosphere's mass, the troposphere is made up of 78 percent nitrogen, 21 percent oxygen, and small amounts of other gases, including carbon dioxide and water vapor.[2]

These life-sustaining gases in the atmosphere are concentrated close to the earth's surface.

The higher up in the troposphere one goes, the less oxygen there is and the colder the temperatures are. On a hot summer day, the temperature at sea level might register 95 degrees Fahrenheit (35 degrees Celsius), while the temperature at the top of the troposphere might be -70 degrees Fahrenheit (-57 degrees Celsius).

The next layer, the stratosphere, stretches from the top of the troposphere to about 31 miles above the ground. The ozone layer is located within the stratosphere.

Take a look at Earth's atmosphere from space and the *Endeavor* space shuttle.

Credit: NASA

In the International Space Station (ISS), 15 countries work together to learn more about space and our home planet. Orbiting at an altitude of 248 miles above Earth, the ISS circles the globe every 90 minutes, moving at a speed of about 17,5000 miles per hour. Take a peek inside.

 NASA Johnson ISS

Ozone molecules protect the earth by absorbing much of the sun's harmful ultraviolet light. As the ozone absorbs the sun's rays, the surrounding temperature rises. The farther from the troposphere layer you are in the stratosphere, the warmer it is.

Because the stratosphere is calmer than the troposphere, with fewer updrafts and less turbulence, it is an ideal place for commercial aircraft to fly. A jet stream flows near the border of the troposphere and the stratosphere. A high-speed flow of air, the jet stream flows from west to east and often brings weather with it.

The International Space Station

Credit: NASA

The mesosphere extends to 53 miles above the earth's surface. It is very cold, with temperatures dropping to -130 degrees Fahrenheit (-90 degrees Celsius). The air is too thin to breathe, and the air pressure is below 1 percent of that found at sea level. Meteors are burned up in this layer before they can reach the earth. That's what you see when you spot a shooting star!

Above the mesosphere, the thermosphere stretches up to 621 miles above the ground. Because it absorbs high-energy X-rays and UV radiation, this layer is incredibly hot, especially near the top. Temperatures reach between 932 degrees Fahrenheit (500 degrees Celsius) and 3,632 degrees Fahrenheit (2000 degrees Celsius).

In many ways, the mesosphere is more like outer space than the atmosphere. Satellites and the International Space Station (ISS) orbit within this layer.

> The aurora borealis (northern lights) and aurora australis (southern lights) occur in the mesosphere, too.

The exosphere is the uppermost layer of the atmosphere. Some scientists don't even consider it to be part of our atmosphere. There is no clear-cut boundary between our atmosphere and space, although some definitions put the top of the atmosphere at about 6,200 miles above the earth. Many satellites orbit the earth in this layer. Each satellite has its own mission and was launched into space on a rocket.

BAROMETER INVENTOR

Italian physicist and mathematician Evangelista Torricelli (1608–1647) discovered how to measure air pressure by inventing the barometer around 1644. Torricelli was working in Florence, Italy, as an assistant to Galileo Galilei (1564–1642), who was experimenting with creating a vacuum in a pipe. After Galileo died, Torricelli continued work on the experiment, though he switched it up a bit. In doing so, he discovered something that he wasn't even looking for! He learned that air had weight and that the instrument he was working on demonstrated just that. The first barometer was created! Torricelli wrote to a colleague on June 11, 1644, "We live immersed at the bottom of a sea of elemental air, which by experiment, undoubtedly has weight." This was a new and profound insight.[3]

AIR PRESSURE

As you walk around, drive to school, or sit at the kitchen table, there is pressure on you the entire time. Although you can't see it and you can't gather it up in your hand, the air around you takes up space and has weight. We call the weight air pressure.

> Walking around on Earth is like walking around at the bottom of the ocean.

The deeper you go and the more water there is above you, the greater the weight pressing down on you. When you are standing on the earth's surface, in a way you are standing under an ocean of air. If you live at sea level, about 60 miles worth of air is above you. Scientists calculate that to be about 15 pounds per square inch of air pressing down on every part of your body.

Why don't you get squashed under all of this air pressure? As the air is pressing on you, the fluids and bones and organs in your body are also pressing out. The pressure on the inside pushing out is equal to the pressure on the outside pushing in. You, as well as all living things on Earth, are in a state of pressure equilibrium. Because of this, everything is balanced.

UNEVEN HEATING

Before it makes it to Earth's surface, much of the sun's radiation is absorbed by ozone molecules or clouds. In addition, some of that energy is reflected back into space by ice and snow.

Meteorologists measure air pressure with an instrument called a barometer. Changes in air pressure signal a change in the weather. Rising air pressure, or high pressure, means that good weather is on the way. Low pressure means stormy days are ahead.

WEATHER WISDOM

One reason that astronauts wear spacesuits is to maintain a normal air pressure on their bodies because space is a vacuum. Without their suits, the pressure from inside their bodies would be greater than the pressure on the outside and their bodies would begin to expand.

Low density of
incident rays
(northern winter)

Earth

Night Equator Day

Sun

High density of
incident rays
(southern summer)

When the sun's rays do hit the earth, the heat is absorbed and then released. This warms the air above the earth.

Not surprisingly, the heating of the earth's surface is not the same everywhere.

Have you ever wondered why the equator is always hot and the North and South Poles are always cold? Just geography, right? Well actually, it's a combination of geography and the fact that the earth is round and tilted at a 23.4-degree angle.

The sun's rays beam out in parallel lines. If the earth was flat, those rays would heat all parts of Earth equally because they would hit all parts equally. However, since the earth is a sphere, the sun's rays hit different parts of the earth at different angles.

The sun's rays hit the equator straight on, giving it concentrated heat. They hit the North and South Poles at an angle, however, so that the heat is spread out across a greater distance and area.

The tilt of the earth also causes the seasons. In the year it takes for the earth to rotate around the sun, the radiation that hits the equator stays consistent. However, because of the tilt, for one half of the year, the Northern Hemisphere receives more of the sun's heat, while the Southern Hemisphere receives more of the sun's heating benefits in the second half of the year.

> The type of surface where the sun's radiation lands also determines how much heat is absorbed and released.

Water heats more slowly than land and it also releases heat more slowly. On the land, forests, sand, and bare soil, such as plowed fields, absorb more radiation than snow and ice.

It is this uneven heating of the earth that causes the uneven heating of the air above the earth. This in turn causes atmospheric movement, which is the beginning of all the weather that we experience, from the calmest, blue-sky winter day to the wildest, windiest hurricane.

KEY QUESTIONS

- **Why might a book about the weather begin with a discussion about the sun?**
- **How can scientists know that the moon was once a part of Earth?**
- **What is the relationship between the atmosphere and the temperature on land?**

SEEING IS BELIEVING

Air takes up space, has weight, and applies pressure. There is an old saying, "Seeing is believing," and it follows that if you don't see, or feel, air pressure, it is hard to remember that it is there. Conduct the experiments below in order to see the effects of air pressure. Use caution with the boiling water.

- **Fill a small glass one-third full of water.** Put an index card over the top of the glass, covering the entire opening of the glass. While holding the index card in place, turn the glass upside down. Carefully remove your hand from the index card. What happens? Why?

- **Put about an inch of water in an empty soda can.** Put the can into a pot filled with about an inch or two of water. Bring the water to a boil. Prepare a shallow pie pan with a small amount of water and ice. When the soda can starts emitting steam, use a pair of tongs to carefully remove the can from the pot and quickly turn it upside down into the dish of ice water. What happens? Why?

- **Tightly stuff a paper towel into the bottom of a glass jar.** Invert the jar into a flat-bottomed, shallow bowl full of water. Wait for a few seconds and then lift the jar straight up out of the water. Feel the paper towel. What do you observe?

> **To investigate more,** consider the inventions that use air pressure that are all around you. Spend some time looking for some these. Are you surprised by any?

Ideas for Supplies ▼

- large rubber balloon
- wide-mouthed jar, such as a canning jar
- rubber band
- straw
- tape
- shoebox

CREATE YOUR OWN BAROMETER

Evangelista Torricelli created the first barometer and used it to see when air pressure was changing. Now it is your turn to make a barometer.

- **Cut the narrow neck off the balloon and carefully stretch it over the mouth of the jar, using a rubber band to hold it in place.** Lay the straw flat on the top of the balloon with its end resting in the middle. Tape it in place.

- **Put the jar into the shoebox with the straw pointing at but not touching the side.** Mark where the straw is pointing on the side of the box. When the straw points up above the starting point, the air pressure is going up. When it points below the starting point, the air pressure is dropping.

- **Check and chart the movement of the straw as it relates to its starting point at the same time twice a day.** Did it point up? Did it stay the same? Did it point down? What does the movement of the straw have to do with air pressure? After you've been tracking the changes in air pressure for several days, check for trends. Does time of day affect air pressure? Does temperature?

> **To investigate more,** when you record the barometric reading, also record the outside temperature on your chart. Do you see any patterns or relationships between barometric pressure and temperature? What were they and what is the correlation?

Chapter 2 ▶
Wind: Air in Motion

AIR: THE INVISIBLE FORCE THAT SHAPES THE WORLD AROUND US!

What causes wind?

Wind is simply the movement of air caused by changes in air pressure and temperature due to the uneven heating of the earth.

Wind—you can't see it, but you can see what it does! Wind helps plants reproduce by dispersing seeds and carrying pollen from one plant to another. It cools you off on a hot, sunny day or makes you feel colder on a chilly one. Wind can save a neighborhood or forest by abruptly changing the direction of a wildfire, or large gusts can push that same fire over dry land at great speeds.

Wind surfers, sailors, and paragliders depend on the wind for fun and speed. Birds use the wind to gain height and save energy as they fly long distances. And speaking of energy, wind generates electricity when it turns the blades of a wind turbine.

Wind blows sand and dust from the Sahara Desert in Africa to faraway lands. Wind blowing over a flooded area can dry it out, sending the extra water back into the atmosphere—but, blowing over the ocean, it can also create destructive waves as tall as mountains.

Think for a moment about what else wind can do. It moves clouds. It bends trees. It makes wind chimes sing and whistles in through cracks in your door. It steals your hat and messes up your hair.

We hear it. We feel it. Sometimes, we can even smell it. But what causes wind in the first place?

In Chapter 1, you learned about the basic ingredients of weather—the sun, the atmosphere, air pressure, and the uneven heating of the earth's surface. As you will see in this chapter, these factors work together to create wind.

THE MOVEMENT OF AIR

Air is made up of gas molecules. Their movement is determined by temperature and air pressure. In cold air, the molecules move slowly and are densely packed together. As air molecules warm up, they move faster and spread out, causing the air to become less dense. Cool air is denser than warm air.

The sun heats the earth's surfaces unevenly, causing some areas to be warmer than others. Here's why that's important. The uneven heating of the earth's different surfaces creates uneven heating of the air above those surfaces. When a pocket of air becomes warmer than the surrounding air, it becomes less dense. That warm air rises, leaving behind a low-pressure area at ground level. The surrounding cooler air, which is denser, moves in to fill that empty space.

The circulation of warm air rising and cool air sinking is called convection. Convection currents occur over large areas of the earth's surface, with large masses of warm air rising and cool air masses moving in to take their place. Convection currents can also occur over small, local areas.

credit: NOAA Geostationary Satellite Server

A satellite image showing two low-pressure systems

THUMBS UP?

Weather maps often show high- and low-pressure areas. Pointing your thumb in the direction indicated by the barometric movement is a simple way to remember what each one means. When you see the high-pressure symbol or hear that the air pressure is rising, point your thumb up. It's going to be a thumbs-up day because good weather is on the way. If you see that the barometric pressure is going down or a low-pressure system is moving in, point your thumb down. Incoming weather gets a thumbs-down.

Wind is caused by the movement of air from a high-pressure area to a low-pressure one. The greater the pressure difference between the two areas and the closer they are together, the faster the air moves and the higher the wind speed or velocity.

Eventually, the heated air cools as it rises higher into the atmosphere. When it is the same temperature as the surrounding air, it stops rising, cools, and sinks back down to Earth, causing a high-pressure area as it presses down on the air below it.

Changes in air pressure signal
changes in weather.

Meteorologists measure the air pressure with a barometer, which records the pressure of the air at the earth's surface. The denser the air, the higher the air pressure. The less dense the air, the lower the pressure.

THE SCIENCE OF WEATHER AND CLIMATE | CHAPTER TWO

Meteorologists know that when the barometric pressure goes up, good weather is usually on the way. Low pressure, on the other hand often means stormy days are ahead.

AIR MASS MOVEMENT

An air mass is a huge body of air with the same temperature and moisture content throughout. Some air masses stretch out for hundreds or thousands of miles across the earth's surface, reaching up to the top of the troposphere. The area over which an air mass forms determines the amount of moisture it contains, as well as its temperature and air pressure.

When the air mass stays put, the weather in that area stays the same. Things change when the air mass moves. Air mass movement can be caused by convection, which causes changes in air pressure, or by wind in the upper atmosphere.

> The main regions of the world that are sources for air masses are the hot areas surrounding the equator and the cold areas around the poles.

Air masses that form over land are dry and are called continental air masses. Those that form over water are moist and are called maritime air masses.

Air masses are defined by the general temperature of the surface over which they are formed. Arctic air masses are very cold. Polar air masses are not as cold as Arctic air masses. Tropical air masses originate over areas around the equator, so they are warm.

An older style of barometer

credit: Collection of Auckland Museum Tamaki Paenga Hira, col.2748, (CC BY 4.0)

A change in barometric pressure lets a weather forecaster know that the weather is about to change. If you carried a barometer up to the top of a mountain, the barometric pressure would change, not because the weather is changing but because the higher you go in the atmosphere, the fewer the air molecules and the lower the air pressure. But what if you carried a barometer on an airplane, which is pressurized so that the passengers aren't affected by the changes in pressure due to altitude? Would the barometer change its reading? Check out a quick explanation at this website.

PS

How Stuff pressure flight

GLOBAL AIR CURRENTS

Global air currents are one way the earth redistributes heat from the equator and cold from the poles to different places around the world. This circulation of warm and cold air is accomplished by six global convection cells—three in the Northern Hemisphere and three in the Southern Hemisphere.

The sun's heat at the equator produces humid, hot air masses that rise and move toward the North and South Poles, leaving behind an area of low pressure. At the same time, the cold air masses in the polar regions flow toward the equator to fill in the low-pressure area that the warm air leaves behind. This cycle is repeated, and an ongoing wind pattern is formed.

The Hadley cell is the largest convection cell. This cell forms when the hot, moist air at the equator rises, leaving behind a band of clouds and low-pressure called the Intertropical Convergence Zone (ITCZ). The rising air reaches heights of 6 to 9 miles above the earth's surface before it begins to spread out toward both poles.

The ITCZ is the band of bright white clouds that cuts across the center of the image.

credit: NASA

As the ITCZ travels, it loses its moisture, gradually cools, and descends to the earth's surface around the latitude of 30 degrees north and south, where it creates a band of high pressure. Upon reaching the earth's surface, the cool, dry air flows back in the direction of the equator, where it is warmed once again, and the pattern repeats itself.

The polar cells at the North and South Poles are the smallest cells, and begin with a high-pressure, cold, dry air mass. Since high pressure always moves toward low pressure, this cold air mass flows in the direction of the equator. Staying close to the earth's surface, the air mass gradually warms up along the way. Eventually, when it reaches the latitudes of about 60 degrees north or south, the warmed polar air mass rises, creating a band of low pressure before it circulates back to a pole.

The Ferrel cell circulates in the midlatitudes, between 35 degrees and 60 degrees north and south. Its circulation of air isn't dependent on temperature. Instead, it circulates air in the opposite direction to the Hadley cell and the polar cells, working like a gear to keep the air moving between them in the form of predictable wind currents. Cold and warm air masses often meet in the midlatitudes, so it is an area with more extreme weather.[1]

CORIOLIS EFFECT

The spinning of the earth affects the flow of the wind at its surface. Imagine you are trying to roll a ball in a straight line from the outer edge of a spinning merry-go-round to a friend in the middle. The ball wouldn't go in a straight line. Because of the spinning of the merry-go-round, the ball would veer off course.

Take a look at global air currents on this interactive map of the world. What information can you glean from this map? Can you distinguish the different cells?

🔍 global air currents earth

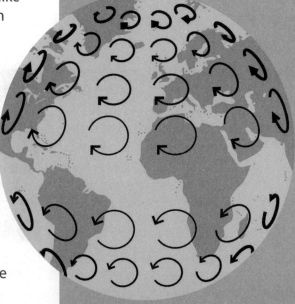

The Coriolis effect, with the six convection cells. Can you spot the Hadley cells and the Ferrel cells?

In the same way, the spinning of the earth causes winds to veer off their straight-line paths, sending them to the right of their intended destination in the Northern Hemisphere and to the left in the Southern Hemisphere.

This is called the Coriolis effect. It is the cause of the individual bands of wind forming in the six convection cells. In the Hadley cell, the winds blow near the earth's surface from east to west, toward the low-pressure zone of the equator.

These steady winds are called the trade winds, or the easterlies.

Blowing from the west to the east in the Ferrel cell, the gusty westerlies blow between the high-pressure bands toward the low-pressure bands.

Finally, the polar winds blow from the high-pressure areas found at both poles toward the low-pressure band north and south. The direction and intensity of these winds form predictable patterns, moving air masses around the globe and affecting the weather.

WEATHER WISDOM

Blowing wind shapes our planet. Sastrugi is the word for the irregular furrows and ridges made from wind erosion on a snowy surface.

WHEN AIR MASSES MEET, WEATHER HAPPENS

Global winds blowing. Giant air masses moving. The Coriolis effect pushing. What is the result of all this rising and sinking, blowing and moving? Stormy weather! And where does a lot of this stormy weather happen? In the midlatitudes, where the warm air masses from the equator meet the cold air masses from the poles.

Air masses are in constant motion, driven by the pressure differences caused by the uneven heating of the earth. Their movement is also determined by the Coriolis effect and winds high in the atmosphere called the jet stream. As air masses move away from their source regions, they bump into each other. And when they do, they don't gently intermingle. They fight for control of the surface below them.

The boundary, or line, where different types of air masses battle, is called a front. The bigger the differences in temperature and pressure between two air masses, the bigger the clash. That difference, that refusal to mix and mingle, causes the most dramatic changes in the weather.

A cold front happens when a cold air mass slams into a warm air mass. The heavier, colder air wedges under the lighter warm air, forcing the warm air to rise quickly into the upper atmosphere. This causes an unsettled area of low pressure along the front, or boundary line, between the cold and warm air masses.

Trade winds got their name because their predictable, steady nature made life easy for sailors from Europe and Africa who were pursuing trade with the Americas.

A cold front meeting a warm front over Lake Michigan
credit: Rachel Kramer (CC By 2.0)

Listen to a meteorologist discuss what happens when weather fronts collide.

Ryan Tidwell-Davidson fronts

Thanks to the wind chill factor, wind on a cold day makes the air feel much colder than what the temperature really is. The stronger the wind, the colder it feels. So, a day with a 30-degree Fahrenheit (-11 degree Celsius) temperature and a wind of 25 miles per hour will actually feel like 16 degrees Fahrenheit (-8.9 degrees Celsius).

At the surface, temperatures plunge, and gusty winds blow. As the warm air rises, it cools and creates clouds and, if there is enough moisture, rain or snow. Behind the cold front, the sky is clear and the weather is calm.

A warm front occurs when a warm air mass meets or overtakes a cold air mass. In a warm front, the lighter, warmer air gently glides over the top of the cold air mass, cooling slowly. Warm fronts often bring light rain and cloudy skies for several days. However, after the front passes, the air stays warm, and some fluffy clouds remain.

A stationary front happens when two air masses meet and neither one gets the upper hand. So, the front stays in place as the air masses continue to bump against each for several days. The weather under the warm air mass may experience a heat wave while the area under the cold air mass may be experiencing colder than normal temperatures. The weather under the front itself will be stormy and unsettled.

> The two air masses battle it out until one wins or they both dissolve.

What happens when more than two air masses come together? An occluded front! Here, a very fast cold front catches up with a slower moving warm front that was busy taking over a different cold front. The warm front gets squashed between the two cold fronts and gets pushed completely off the ground.

A wide variety of weather can be found at the boundary of an occluded front, but that weather is not usually severe.

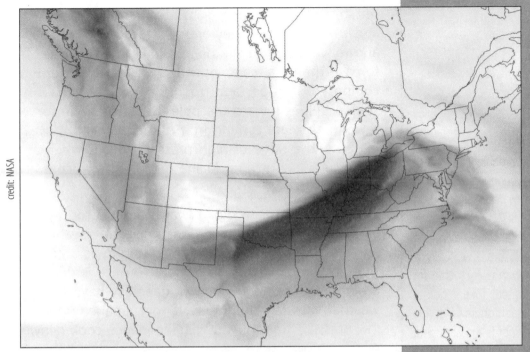

credit: NASA

In this aerial image, you can see the jet stream dipping through the United States, bringing frigid air from Canada into the lower states.

JET STREAMS

Fast-moving jet streams are another type of global wind that affects the weather. These jet streams blow high in the atmosphere. There are four jet streams, two in each hemisphere, each blowing along the boundaries between cold and hot air masses.

The polar jet is the strongest, located around the latitudes of 60 degrees north and south, while the subtropical jet is located around 30 degrees north and south. The air flows from high to low pressure, which causes high winds. The bigger the difference in the temperature, the bigger the difference in the pressure and the stronger the wind.

The Beaufort scale is a system for measuring wind created in 1805 by Frances Beaufort (1774–1857), an Irish Royal Navy officer, as a navigation tool for sailors. Eventually, a scale was created for land, too. Take a look at the Beaufort scale at this website. What is the strongest wind you've experienced?

 Beaufort scale

Jet streams are stronger in winter than in spring and summer, when they are said to "follow the sun" and move closer to the poles. Blowing from west to east, the jet streams flow in a wave-like pattern composed of ridges and troughs. When the jet stream bulges toward the poles, it leaves room for a warm air mass coming from the equator to move in, forming a ridge of high pressure. This is when a place such as northern Maine might experience a heat wave.

When the jet stream dips toward the equator, a cold air mass from the polar regions moves in, creating a low-pressure trough. This might show up as a cold snap in Florida. If the area where you live is under a high-pressure ridge, you will generally have warm weather with fair conditions. If your area is under a low-pressure trough, you will experience cool, rainy, or snowy conditions.

Jet stream winds can be many miles wide and deep and reach speeds of more than 275 miles per hour. The shape of a jet stream resembles a flattened tube. The fastest winds occur at the core of the jet stream, decreasing toward its edges. So, the wind speed at the core might be 140 miles per hour, while at the edges, it might be 80 miles per hour.

LOCAL WINDS

The movement of air is also influenced by local landforms and surface characteristics. Local winds cover small areas. While the strength and direction of global winds is continuous and predictable, the strength and direction of local winds varies, and their lifespan is short.

Both global and local winds are caused by the uneven heating of the earth's surface.

Just as large-scale convection currents cause global winds, small-scale convection currents cause local winds. Sea breezes, or onshore breezes, are local winds found along coastlines. On a sunny day, the air over the land heats up faster than the air above the ocean. The warmer land air rises and the cooler sea air sweeps in to replace it.

Land breezes, or offshore breezes, are caused because water retains the sun's heat longer than the land. In the evening, once the sun goes down, the air over the water is warmer than the air over the land. The warm air over the water rises and the cooler land air rushes in to replace it.

Another common local wind is called an anabatic wind, which is caused when the side of a mountain or a steep hill is heated by the sun. The air directly above the slope is warmer than the adjacent air. The warm air rises along the side of the mountain, creating an upslope wind.

Glider pilots look for anabatic winds to increase their altitude. On the flip side, cyclists racing down the side of a mountain don't like anabatic winds because they slow down the cyclists' speeds.

In the evening or on cloudy days, the mountainside is no longer receiving the heat of the sun's rays. Downslope or katabatic winds are created when the air higher up the slope loses heat faster than the air in the adjacent valley.

READING THE WIND

An instrument called an anemometer measures wind speed. On a weather map, wind speed is indicated by wind barbs that spread out from high-pressure centers, which are marked with a capital H, and low-pressure centers, marked with a capital L.

Here is a weather map with high- and low-pressure systems marked and isobars showing the pressure gradient.

 climate isobars isotherms image

The farther apart the lines are, the less difference there is between the high and low pressure and the lower the wind speed.

Wind direction is indicated by the area from which the wind blows. If the weather forecast states that there is a northwest wind, you know the wind is blowing from the northwest toward the southeast.

Wind is a powerful force of nature. Without it, much of the earth would be too hot or too cold to live. But, thanks to the wind's constant movement, warm and cold air are constantly being redistributed around the globe to keep the temperatures in most areas conducive to life.

In the next chapter, we will see what happens when we add water to this weather mix.

Since early times, people have been harnessing wind energy. Today, wind turbines are used to convert wind power into electric energy. Wind is a renewable energy that is cleaner to use than oil or coal. Take a look at wind energy in this video.

 science 360 power wind

KEY QUESTIONS

- **What causes wind?**
- **Why does warm air rise and cold air sink?**
- **How do global winds form? What is their effect on the earth's weather and climate?**
- **Can you name two types of fronts and explain what they are?**

MAKE YOUR OWN ANEMOMETER

Since wind is one of the key ingredients in the creation of weather, avid weather watchers measure its speed and direction. An anemometer is an essential tool for tracking the wind. You can make your own and use it for your observations.

- **Find the center of the plate.** Draw two perpendicular lines through it.

- **Using two-sided tape or a stapler, attach four cups to the plate at each point where drawn lines meet the edge.** The cups should be on their sides with the opening of each facing in the same direction. Mark one of the cups with a marker.

- **Push the pin in through the center of the plate.** Push it all the way through into the pencil's eraser.

- **Hold the cup anemometer outside and have a partner count how many times it goes around in 30 seconds.** How fast is it spinning? Which direction is the wind coming from? Record your observations in your science journal. How can you use the information to help predict weather?

> **To investigate more,** try to determine the general speed of the wind using a guesstimate. Suppose you counted that the anemometer spun around 15 times in a minute and, according to your best guess, the wind was blowing at 10 miles per hour. You then know that 15 spins in a minute equal winds of about 10 miles per hour. Can you think of any other way to calibrate your anemometer?

Inquire & Investigate

Ideas for Supplies ▼

- sturdy paper plate
- pencil
- two-sided tape or a stapler
- 4 small paper cups
- push pin
- stopwatch
- weather journal

Want to learn more about anemometers? Check out this website!

PS

Explain stuff anemometers

PUTTING IT ALL TOGETHER

Perhaps you've heard the saying, "A picture is worth a thousand words." You've just read lots of words explaining how wind and temperature and the earth's tilt work together to make the weather. Now is your chance to create your own "picture" by labeling these different parts on a map.

- **Use the information you learned from this chapter.** Label the low- and high-pressure bands in both hemispheres on a map of the United States that shows latitude.

- **Draw the direction of the wind in the six global convection cells.** Label each one.

- **Put in the air mass source regions.** Label each one.

- **Using a map or your own travel knowledge, identify cities within these different latitudes.** What do you know about the weather in these different regions? How does it relate to the information from the chapter? Does it fit in with the wind and weather patterns you've read about? How?

> **To investigate more,** go through the same process using a world map. What can this tell you about the weather in different locations around the world?

VOCAB LAB

Write down what you think each word means. What root words can you find to help you? What does the context of the word tell you?

anemometer, convection, dense, front, predictable, and **trough.**

Compare your definitions with those of your friends or classmates. Did you all come up with the same meanings? Turn to the text and glossary if you need help.

Chapter 3 ▶
Just Add Water

What role does
water play in the
creation of weather?

Water is an essential ingredient in weather. Traveling in all three states (solid, liquid, and gas) as it moves through the water cycle, it is necessary for life on this planet.

Water shapes our world in a very real sense. A river carved out the Grand Canyon in Arizona and glaciers gouged out the valleys in California's Yosemite National Park. Flooding reroutes rivers and unexpected rainstorms can bring a dry desert into blossom. And speaking of changing shape, water not only changes the shape of the earth, water itself is constantly changing.

Did you know that water is the only substance on Earth that occurs naturally in all three states? As a solid, it exists as permanent ice in icebergs and glaciers. As a liquid, it fills oceans, runs through rivers, and even swishes around below your feet in natural underground reservoirs. Finally, water vapor is an invisible gas that is abundant in our atmosphere. You are breathing it in . . . and out . . . right now!

And although the state of water is always changing as it circulates around the planet, the amount of water on the planet is largely unchanged.

Think about it—the water in your glass right now might have spent time frozen in an iceberg floating near the North Pole or submerged in the depths of the ocean for hundreds of years before it was recycled and cleaned by a huge but efficient recycling system: the earth's water cycle.

From solid to liquid to gas and back again, water is an essential ingredient to life on Earth.

Due to its "just right" position in the solar system, the earth has large amounts of water, not only in the atmosphere but on the surface and even below the surface. To put it simply, without water, there wouldn't be life on Earth.

Earth has so much water that its nickname is the Blue Planet.

THE EVER-CHANGING WATER MOLECULE

We can see that water is essential, but what is it actually made of? Water molecules consist of two hydrogen atoms and one oxygen atom, and they are constantly moving. Much like air molecules, their movement is dependent on temperature. The molecular formula for water is H_2O.

Water molecules have both a positive and a negative charge, and these charges, positive in one molecule to negative in another, are what attracts individual water molecules to other water molecules, allowing them to form hydrogen bonds. These bonds determine the different states of water.

WEATHER WISDOM

Due to climate change and population growth, our supplies of useable water are being rapidly depleted. Some regions, such as parts of India, are already experiencing desperate water shortages.

Every time you breathe out, you are breathing out water vapor, which is then put into circulation in the water cycle. Breathe onto a mirror to see the water vapor condense into tiny water droplets.

In its liquid state, water molecules are actively moving and bouncing around, constantly making and breaking hydrogen bonds. When water heats up, the molecules move even faster, until some of them break away and float into the air as water vapor. They have changed into a different state of matter.

On the flip side of the thermometer, as ice forms, the molecules connect into six-sided ice crystals. They then connect to other ice crystals, forming a 3-dimensional lattice—ice! This creates more space between each molecule. For this reason, ice is less dense and weighs less than water in its liquid form.

THREE STATES OF WATER

Ice covers the coldest parts of the earth's surface and has been frozen there for thousands and thousands of years. As water freezes into ice, it expands. As it expands, it can split rocks, slowly carve out mountain valleys, and burst pipes in your basement.

The world's large ice sheets play an important role in keeping Earth in the "just right" Goldilocks zone. For one thing, they help balance the earth's temperature by reflecting some of the sun's heat back into space. In addition, permanent ice stores about 75 to 79 percent of the earth's fresh water. Unfortunately, climate change is causing the permanent ice covering the earth to melt. And, as more ice melts, more heat is being absorbed by the earth's surface and less fresh water is being stored.

Liquid water is used for more than drinking, bathing, and cooking, although those are important daily uses. Massive amounts of water are also used to grow our food, to run hydroelectric plants, and as an important part of manufacturing, to name just a few uses.

A hydroelectric dam

Liquid water, like ice, plays an important part in keeping the earth's temperatures "just right." Warm and cool water continuously circulates around the planet, creating a balance in the earth's climate system.

Water in its gaseous form is called water vapor, or humidity. It is abundant in our atmosphere. Although you can't see it, if the atmosphere has enough water vapor, you can feel it on your skin. The amount of water vapor in the atmosphere varies greatly, depending on the earth's latitude, with much of the water vapor supplied by oceans near the tropics. It is never completely absent from the atmosphere, even in the driest desert.

THE WATER CYCLE

When surface water is heated by the sun, it evaporates, or changes into water vapor, and floats up into the air. The water vapor rises until it reaches the dew point, or the point where the cooler temperatures cause it to condense into microscopic water droplets. If enough of these water droplets are around, a cloud forms.

WEATHER WISDOM

The National Snow and Ice Data Center reports that if all the land ice melted, the ocean level would rise 230 feet worldwide. Would that affect the city you live in or near?

Did you know that liquid water can dissolve more substances than any other liquid, including sulfuric acid? Or that it takes about 70 gallons of water to fill a bathtub? Read these and other fascinating water facts here.

 seametrics water

A rising mass of air cools at a rate of 5.4 degrees Fahrenheit (9.8 degrees Celsius) per 1,000 feet. If the air mass remains warmer than the surrounding air, it will continue to rise. Stable air is air that is no longer rising, while unstable air is still going up.[1]

Eventually, as the droplets join, they become too heavy to remain aloft in the air. The water falls back to the earth as precipitation, to be absorbed by the soil or rocks, seep deep into the ground, become ice, or return to rivers, lakes, and oceans. When precipitation is absorbed by plants through their roots, it is released back into the air through their foliage in a process called transpiration.

CLOUD FORMATION

From fluffy white masses floating gently across a summer sky to dark stormy towers to layers of gray blocking out the sun, there are many kinds of clouds. No matter what shape they take, clouds are an essential part of our weather system, circulating life-giving water throughout the earth.

Clouds form when water vapor in the atmosphere reaches the dew point. However, in order to do that, the water vapor attaches to microscopic dust and pollen particles called condensation nuclei and condenses to microscopic water droplets. Millions of these water droplets make up clouds, which move around the globe collecting more water vapor along the way. As more and more water droplets float around in a cloud, they bump into each other, join, and form bigger and bigger water droplets in a process called coalescence.

Finally, when the water droplets become too heavy to float, they fall as precipitation.

All clouds form through condensation, and convection is one way this happens. Convection clouds include cumulus, cumulonimbus, and stratocumulus.

Orographic clouds are formed when an air mass traveling near the earth's surface bumps into a mountain slope or some other sort of high landform. The air is forced up the slope and, as it reaches the top, it cools and condenses, forming a cloud. The wind may carry it away, or, if the cloud holds enough moisture, precipitation occurs on the upslope side of the hill or mountain before it descends on the other side. Lenticular clouds are formed in this way.

Frontal clouds form at weather fronts. This is where two air masses meet at the earth's surface and one is pushed up into the air. Frontal clouds may spread out over large areas and often are so big that they fill the sky and block out the sun.

CLOUD CLASSIFICATION

When identifying clouds, weather forecasters look at two things—their shape and their altitude. The shape and the altitude of a cloud hint at the weather to come.

Often, the names of clouds identify both their shapes and their locations in the atmosphere.

The four basic shapes of clouds are cirrus, cumulus, stratus, and nimbus. Cirrus clouds are feathery, wispy clouds made up of ice crystals. Cumulus clouds are rounded, fluffy clouds with flat bases that form at the altitude where rising water vapor condenses. When you see large layers or sheets of clouds covering the sky, you are probably seeing stratus clouds. These signal a grey, drizzly, or snowy day. Finally, nimbus clouds are the dark clouds that start low in the atmosphere and carry lots of moisture.

To fully understand a cloud, you must also know if it is a high-level, mid-level, or low-level cloud. Altitude determines a cloud's characteristics.

High-level clouds always include "cirrus" in their name. High-altitude clouds form near the very top of the troposphere, between 20,000 and 46,000 feet, where the winds are much faster than below. Because of this, cirrus clouds tend to be the fastest moving of all clouds. Since the water vapor didn't condense until it was high in the atmosphere, cirrus clouds are formed from ice crystals. They are often considered good-weather clouds.

There are three main types of high-level clouds: cirrus, cirrocumulus, and cirrostratus.

Cirrostratus and stratocumulus clouds

HOW MUCH?

Traditionally, cloud cover has been measured in oktas. Meteorologists look at the sky, mentally divide it in eighths, and decide how many eighths of the sky is covered in clouds. Zero oktas mean the sky is clear. Eight oktas mean it is completely covered. How many oktas do you see outside right now?

The mid-level clouds have names that begin with the Latin word *alto*, which means "high," even though they are mid-level. The bases of mid-level clouds are found at a height of 6,500 to 20,000 feet. The two main types of mid-level clouds are altocumulus and altostratus. These clouds are formed mainly of water droplets but might also contain ice crystals. Their appearance signals the appearance of rain or snow.

Low-level clouds have a base that lies below 6,500 feet. They can be small and fluffy or huge, towering storm clouds called cumulonimbus. The mist and fog that sometimes form at ground level are also considered low-level clouds.

The ability to identify clouds is an important part of predicting the weather. But aside from the scientific benefits, clouds are just beautiful to look at. Take a few minutes to enjoy their magnificence. If you want to try to identify them, give it a shot!

 Nat Geo clouds gallery

PRECIPITATION

Any moisture that falls from clouds is considered to be precipitation. The type of precipitation that falls is determined by the temperature of the cloud it came from as well as the temperature of the air it falls through.

Did you know that you can make snow? Ski areas depend on snow for their business, and they figured out a way to make it when the weather doesn't give it to them. Big machines spray a fine mist of water droplets—often also containing a mix of condensation nuclei—into the air. Once the mist reaches the air, the cold temperatures do the rest of the work. And, voilà, instant snow!

When the air is very humid, it is harder for your body to cool down when it's hot. The more humidity in the air, the less your sweat evaporates from your skin, so the less cooling you experience.

When the air temperature of the cloud is above 32 degrees Fahrenheit (0 degrees Celsius), rain forms. As the millions of tiny water droplets bounce around in the cloud, they bump into each other, coalescing to create bigger and bigger droplets. Eventually, those water droplets get too heavy to stay up in the air and they fall to the ground as rain.

A typical raindrop is about one-tenth of an inch in diameter. It takes millions of water droplets to make a full-sized raindrop.

The air in a cloud below the freezing point of 32 degrees Fahrenheit (0 degrees Celsius) is made up of a mixture of ice crystals and supercooled water droplets, which is water that is cooled below freezing but not frozen. The supercooled rain can freeze onto the ice crystals.

As the ice crystals grow, they stick to each other, eventually forming a snowflake. Just like raindrops, when snowflakes get too heavy, they fall. If the air they fall through continues to stay at freezing temperatures, the snowflakes fall to the ground as snow.

Humidity is a measure of how much water vapor is in the air. The warmer the temperature of the air, the more water vapor it can hold. Relative humidity is the amount of water vapor in the air compared to the amount it can hold. The higher the relative humidity, the higher the likelihood of precipitation. When air is completely full of water vapor, it is said to be saturated. When the air is saturated, the water vapor condenses to liquid water.

A foggy Golden Gate Bridge in San Francisco Bay, California

credit: runner310 (CC BY 2.0)

Fog is a cloud that appears on the ground. It is made up of tiny drops of water, but, unlike a cloud, the water comes from a water source close by.

Fog forms when the saturated air cools to its dew point. Sea fog is formed when warm, moist air is cooled over a cold sea. Radiation fog occurs when the ground cools after sunset and cools the air directly above it—causing the air to reach its dew point. Mist is a form of precipitation where the droplets in the fog coalesce to become tiny drops of water just barely heavy enough to fall to the ground.

Have you ever seen dew drops on a leaf early on an autumn morning?

Dew forms when warm water vapor in the air touches a cold surface. The water vapor condenses into dew droplets. Dew is always formed in fog, but it may also form on a clear night when the layer of air touching cold surfaces reaches its dew point, but the air immediately above it does not.

DIFFERENT KINDS OF ICE?

You might have seen rain and hail, but you might not have heard of some types of precipitation! Graupel looks like tiny Styrofoam pellets and forms when supercooled water droplets freeze onto falling snowflakes. Sleet leaves the cloud as snow, but it passes through warm air, turning into partially melted snow and raindrops. When it passes through another layer of below-freezing air closer to the earth's surface, it refreezes into clear ice pellets—sleet. And freezing rain is rain that freezes when it lands on surfaces that are below freezing.

WaPo graupel

The exact same thing happens when you pour a drink into a cold glass and the glass starts to "sweat" or get beads of moisture on it. The water vapor in the air that touches the glass is immediately cooled down to its dew point and condenses.

Frost occurs when the ground or surface temperature is below freezing. Water vapor in the air that touches the frozen surface turns directly to ice, forming soft, white crystals.

THE OCEAN AND ITS CURRENTS

Since it covers 71 percent of the earth, the ocean has a big influence on the health of our planet. As water evaporates from the ocean, the salt is left behind, so the ocean is the main source of the earth's fresh water.

The oceans help clean our air by absorbing carbon dioxide, a greenhouse gas, from the atmosphere. Finally, the ocean plays a major role in keeping the earth's temperatures in balance, through a vast system of interconnected ocean currents that transport warm water from the tropics and cold water from both poles around the world.

How are the world's ocean currents like a fast-moving roller coaster ride? Watch this video and find out.

 Nat Geo ocean currents climate

Currents are like huge rivers flowing through the ocean. They are continuous, cohesive streams of sea water that circulate throughout the globe, steered by the wind and by the placement of the continents. Our oceans have two enormous current systems worldwide—surface currents flow in the thin upper layer of the ocean and deepwater currents circulate along the ocean's floor.

Surface currents are generated by the global winds that flow in predictable patterns due to the earth's spin and the Coriolis effect. As wind blows across the sea, friction drags the top layer of the water into motion, which gets the water beneath it moving as well.

The water's surface currents flow in circular patterns called gyres. Six gyres circle clockwise in the Northern Hemisphere and counterclockwise in the Southern Hemisphere.

When the oceans' current systems are disrupted, the weather changes. Those changes often have a negative impact worldwide. One predictable disruption in ocean currents is called El Niño. Have you ever noticed any effects of El Niño?

 PS

 NOAA El Niño

Ocean surface currents

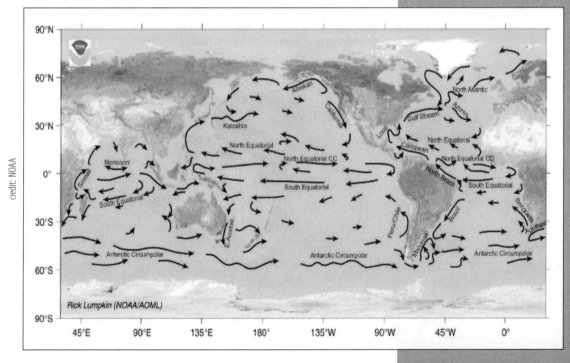

credit: NOAA

The deepwater current is slow but steady, and eventually, as it moves water along this global conveyor belt, it empties one ocean into another during the course of 1,000 years.

Two are in both the Atlantic and Pacific Oceans, one is in the Indian Ocean, and one circles around Antarctica. These surface currents vary in speed and size, but they all affect the weather and climate of the lands that they pass. For instance, the gulf stream current is responsible for the mild climate of Western Europe as compared to other regions at the same latitude.

On the other hand, deepwater currents, also known as thermohaline circulation, form a continual current that functions as a giant conveyor belt as it loops through all the oceans' waters. Starting near Greenland, the surface water is very cold and also saltier because, as sea ice forms, the salt is left behind in the water.

The cold dense water sinks to the ocean's floor and begins to flow south, its course dictated by the presence of continents on each side. The current warms up as it passes the equator. When it eventually reaches Antarctica, more cold water is added, recharging the current's energy. The current continues toward the Indian Ocean and the Pacific, bringing cooler water and cooler air temperatures to warm climates and warmer water and therefore warmer air to cool climates.

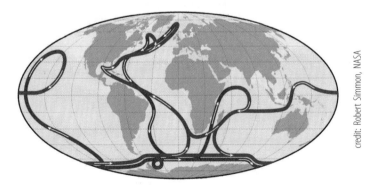

The global path of thermohaline circulation

Red = warm water   Blue = cold water

credit: Robert Simmon, NASA

A map of ocean currents from 1943

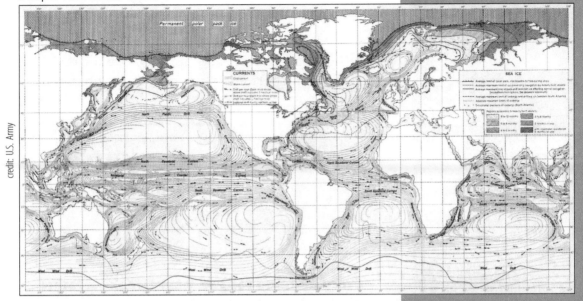

credit: U.S. Army

These global ocean currents affect the climates and local ecosystems of all the land they pass. Scientists are concerned that global warming could alter or disrupt these currents, thus disrupting the positive effects that they provide around the planet.

When you see a photo of Earth from space, you can see why it is often called the Blue Planet. Liquid water colors our world. It's the presence of water, in all its forms, that fuels the water cycle, creates clouds, and sends rivers of currents moving through our oceans.

The surface and deepwater currents balance the earth's temperatures by circulating heat around the world. See how scientists consider ocean currents when trying to recover from an oil spill.

PS

🔍 NOAA oil loop

KEY QUESTIONS

- **How does water move from one state to another?**
- **How do clouds form? Why do they look different from each other?**
- **What purpose do global ocean currents serve?**

Inquire & Investigate

WEATHER LOG

Clouds give lots of clues about the current weather and the weather that is on the way. Use a cloud identification chart and an okta chart to predict the weather.

cloud identification chart

🔍 NASA clouds

okta chart

🔍 Cloud coverage chart

- **Every morning for two weeks, make weather observations and record them in your science journal.** Record precipitation and cloud type and coverage.

- **After identifying the morning cloud type and coverage, make a prediction for the afternoon weather based on that information.** In the afternoon, write down what the actual weather turns out to be.

> **To investigate more,** consider that clouds are always moving. Sometimes, they signal weather on the way, sometimes, they don't. Regardless, clouds are always interesting to watch. Set up a cloud-watching frame by choosing a window or view from your home. During the course of a day, look out through that frame every hour or two. How do the clouds change? Keep a cloud diary. What would happen if you moved the frame to see higher up in the sky? Would the type of clouds differ?

VOCAB LAB 📖

Write down what you think each word means. What root words can you find to help you? What does the context of the word tell you?

altitude, coalescence, condense, dew point, frontal cloud, precipitation, saturated, and **water vapor**.

Compare your definitions with those of your friends or classmates. Did you all come up with the same meanings? Turn to the text and glossary if you need help.

Chapter 4 ▶
Weather on the Wild Side

THUNDERSTORMS, TORNADOES, BLIZZARDS, HURRICANES... OUR EARTH CAN BE AN EXTREME PLACE!

What is extreme weather and how is it different from everyday weather?

Extreme weather is weather that is out of the ordinary. It is weather that causes damage, destruction, and even loss of life.

A tornado rips through a town causing widespread destruction. Anxious families on the coast of Florida watch the news for information of a hurricane several days from shore. Will it veer west and make landfall or will it head north and dissipate? A blizzard strikes on the East Coast. Cities are shut down, millions of people lose their electricity, and, yes, schools are closed.

All weather affects our daily life, but extreme weather upends it. Property damage, dangerous conditions, even death can be the result. And extreme weather's effects often go beyond the storm itself. Airline schedules are interrupted for days. Roads are closed. Crops are destroyed. Vacation spots are no longer habitable. Residents of an area might have to wait weeks for utilities such as electricity and water to be turned back on.

One of the most difficult things about extreme weather is that it is hard to predict. Forecasters know when the conditions are ripe for a tornado, but they can't say where, when, or if it will happen.

Hurricanes build up in the ocean and may be heading for land until, at the very last moment, they veer back out to sea. Or vice versa!

Severe or extreme weather is unpredictable, terrifying, and also, necessary. What? Necessary? Yes! Just as a forest fire serves the purpose of cleaning out a forest to make way for new growth, severe storms are caused, in part, by atmospheric imbalances.

Storms serve to rebalance the atmosphere.

While extreme weather is necessary to the continued health of our planet, there is evidence that the weather has become more extreme in recent years and that this uptick in terrible events is caused by climate change. As with everything else related to the earth, balance is everything.

A hurricane map from 2005 shows how many Atlantic Ocean hurricanes made landfall and how many went out to sea.

WEATHER WISDOM

Wind shear is a difference in the wind speed or direction between two air currents over a relatively short distance in the atmosphere. In the case of a thunderstorm, wind shear is two different wind speeds or directions within the towering cumulonimbus cloud.

THUNDERSTORMS

Thousands of thunderstorms occur every day in the earth's atmosphere. They are most often found in the midlatitudes, with Florida's gulf coast experiencing the greatest number of any place in the United States—an average of 130 days a year!

The life cycle of a thunderstorm has three stages: developing, mature, and dissipating. In the developing stage, a warm air mass forms, rises, and condenses into a cumulus cloud. The energy, or latent heat, created by condensation keeps the air inside the cloud warmer than the air outside the cloud, and therefore makes it unstable. The condensation continues, the updraft persists, and the air continues to rise, building and building into a towering cumulonimbus cloud, reaching the top of the troposphere and then flattening out into its recognizable anvil shape.

The classic anvil shape of a thunderstorm cloud

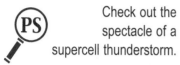

Check out the spectacle of a supercell thunderstorm.

 panhandle supercell thunderstorm

Scientists have detected a link between climate change and extreme weather. The average frequency and intensity of storms has increased in recent years as the temperature of the globe has risen.

Things change, however, during the mature stage of the thunderstorm. Precipitation begins to fall, creating a downdraft. Lightning, thunder, strong winds, heavy rain, and sometimes hail occur as the energy built up in the cloud is released. The dissipating stage begins when falling precipitation cools the air at the ground, shutting off the updrafts of warm air. The air becomes stable. The cloud and energy gradually disappear and the storm is over.

The severest—and rarest—thunderstorm is the supercell. Lasting longer than an hour and feeding off the energy from the updraft, its defining characteristic is the mesocyclone. This is a large, horizontally rotating wind within the storm.

The mesocyclone is the result of wind shear, or the sharp difference between the updraft and downdraft currents. Most tornadoes come from supercells.

LIGHTNING, THUNDER, AND HAIL, OH MY!

As the ice crystals and water droplets are bounced around by the turbulent air inside the thunder cloud, they bump into each other, causing a buildup of static electricity. The heavier, negatively charged ice crystals migrate to the base of the cloud, while the lighter, positively charged ice crystals gather near the top.

> When the charge builds up to a level that the cloud can no longer contain, a lightning bolt of energy occurs between the two charges in the cloud.

LATENT HEAT

Latent heat is the energy or heat released or absorbed when water changes states between liquid, gas, and solid. The amount of heat released by condensation is equal to the amount required to make liquid evaporate. So, if 1 gram of water requires 600 calories of energy to change from liquid water to water vapor, that same amount of energy is released when that water vapor transforms back into water droplets. Are you familiar with the concept that energy cannot be created or destroyed? The same principle applies here. The same amount of energy that goes in is the same amount of energy that comes out. Balance![1]

The updraft speed needs to be at least 37 miles per hour for a thunderstorm to produce a dime-sized hailstone and 56 miles per hour for a golf-ball-sized hailstone.

Lightning can also occur between a negative charge in the cloud and a positive charge on the ground or in another cloud. A bolt of lightning causes the heated air to expand and then contract rapidly. Thunder is the sound of the resulting shock wave.

Another phenomenon that occurs during thunderstorms is hail. How? The air at the top of a thundercloud is below freezing. When strong updrafts push water droplets up to the top of the cloud, they freeze and then drop back down again, getting coated with more water droplets. The hailstones might bounce back and forth between the bottom and top of the cloud many times, growing bigger and bigger with each trip as they are coated with layers of freezing water.

Eventually, the hailstones are spit out of the cloud and fall to the ground. If you cut a hailstone in half and look carefully, you should be able to distinguish a separate layer for each trip up to the top of the cloud. But watch out! Hail can cause a lot of damage to cars, homes, crops—even people!

WEATHER WISDOM

A single stroke of lightning can heat the air around it to 54,000 degrees Fahrenheit (30,000 degrees Celsius). That's five times hotter than the surface of the sun! Since light travels at a rate of 186,000 miles per second, far faster than sound, people see lightning before they hear thunder. A single lightning bolt unleashes as much energy as blowing up a ton of TNT. Needless to say, head inside during a lightning storm. If that's impossible, try to get to low ground and stay away from tall things such as trees and telephone poles.

TORNADOES

Tornadoes are the offspring of thunderstorms and hurricanes. They produce the strongest winds on the planet, up to 300 miles per hour, and can last from a minute up to an hour. They can occur any time of the year if the conditions are right, but mostly happen in the spring or summer.

One of the most dangerous things about tornadoes is their unpredictability. Meteorologists know under what conditions tornadoes are likely to form, but they can't say if they will, or where. Tornadoes are most likely to develop from a supercell thunderstorm from their conditions of unstable air.

As you already learned, in a thundercloud, updrafts and downdrafts are occurring at the same time. This sets up a situation where the competing air currents begin to spin or roll around each other, forming a mesocyclone. At first the spinning is horizontal, but it can easily turn vertical and spin down out of the cloud. When the mesocyclone touches the ground, it is a tornado.

Weak tornadoes might last a few minutes and have winds under 100 miles per hour. More than two-thirds of tornadoes fall into this category. Nearly a third of all tornadoes are categorized as strong, lasting for 20 minutes or longer with winds of 110 to 120 miles per hour. Violent tornadoes are the least common, but can do the most damage. With winds at 205 miles per hour, they are strong enough to toss cars into the air. These violent tornadoes result in the most deaths.

What should you do if you hear a tornado warning? That's easy. Find shelter right away. The best place to ride out the storm is a basement or storm cellar. The next best choice is to get to an interior, windowless room on the lowest level of your house or building. Stay away from doors and outside walls. Finally, cover your head and neck with your arm just in case there is flying debris.

Ready.goc tornado

A tornado north of Solomon, Kansas, in 2016

credit: Ks0stm (CC BY 4.0)

Although tornadoes can occur anywhere in the world, 75 percent of them happen in the United States. Most of those occur in a region that includes Texas, Oklahoma, Kansas, Nebraska, and Missouri. Dubbed "Tornado Alley," the area is susceptible to the creation of tornadoes thanks to its flat landscape. It is a perfect battleground for cold air masses from central Canada, dry air masses from the Rocky Mountains, and warm, wet air masses from the Gulf of Mexico to fight it out. When these large air masses collide, they sometimes form supercell thunderstorms, which can evolve into tornadoes.[2]

A HURRICANE FORMS

Hurricanes take shape in warm oceans off the equator. They can be hundreds of miles wide and stretch 10 miles into the atmosphere. Usually taking several days to develop, they can reach speeds of more than 157 miles per hour.

So how does a hurricane become a hurricane?

In the United States, the official hurricane season is June 1 through November 30, but hurricanes usually occur in the fall, when ocean temperatures are warmest. Starting much like a thunderstorm, the warm air over the ocean rises and condenses to form a cumulus cloud, eventually morphing into a towering cumulonimbus cloud.

On land, a thunderstorm dies out when the cool rain shuts off the updraft. But over the ocean, the warm, moist ocean provides endless fuel to keep the ocean thunderstorm going. The updraft creates a low-pressure system. The surrounding air pours in to fill the void, creating wind. Thanks to the Coriolis effect, the upward air current begins to spin around the low-pressure center—counterclockwise in the Northern Hemisphere and clockwise in the Southern Hemisphere. As the storm is pushed by the trade winds, it joins with other thunderclouds, becoming first a tropical storm and eventually reaching full-fledged hurricane status when wind speeds reach 74 miles per hour.[3]

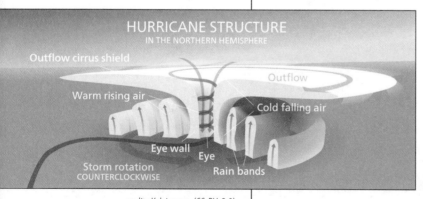

HURRICANE STRUCTURE
IN THE NORTHERN HEMISPHERE

Outflow cirrus shield

Outflow

Warm rising air

Cold falling air

Eye wall

Eye

Storm rotation
COUNTERCLOCKWISE

Rain bands

credit: Kelvinsong (CC BY 2.0)

The eye, or center, of the hurricane can measure up to 40 miles across. In the very low air pressure of the eye, it is eerily calm with little wind or rain. The strongest, most deadly winds blow in the bands of clouds, called the eye wall, that surround the center. Bands of rain extend out from the eye wall.

TRACKING A HURRICANE

Meteorologists use different types of technology to track hurricanes. Satellites send photographs from space as well as measure a hurricane's winds and chart its direction. Special planes fly directly into the hurricane to gather data, such as temperature and wind speed, and an instrument called a dropsonde is dropped from a plane or drone into the hurricane to collect even more information.

After all this information is gathered and analyzed with the help of computer weather models, meteorologists begin to send out watches and warnings. They give city officials and citizens the information they need to prepare in case the hurricane makes landfall.

Hurricane Florence, 2018, from the International Space Station

credit: NASA Goddard Space Flight Center (CC BY 2.0)

The five-point Saffir-Simpson Hurricane Wind Scale rates hurricanes based on their wind speed and gives a list of potential damage for each level. Take a look!

🔍 NHC Saffir-Simpson

At their weakest, hurricane winds blow at 74 miles per hour. This is equal to a car driving fast on a highway. If the wind is blowing at 155 miles per hour, it is barreling through a city at the speed of a fast-moving train.

It is not unusual for hurricanes to switch course at the last minute or for the amount of rain to be more, or less, than expected. Once hurricanes make landfall, their fuel supply of warm moist air is cut off and they die down. Unfortunately, this usually does not occur before they cause immense wind and water damage.

Trees and power lines are knocked down and pieces of buildings and city debris, such as street signs and park benches, fly through the air. Hurricanes carry with them huge amounts of water, and that water falls as rain when the hurricane hits land.

Enormous waves cause additional damage and flooding as they come ashore.

Storm surges are often the greatest source of damage. As the hurricane moves across the ocean, a mound of water forms ahead of it, getting higher and higher as it goes. When the hurricane reaches land, all that water has to go somewhere. It gets pushed up onto the shore in a storm surge. If the storm surge is tall enough, it can flow far inland, causing additional flooding and damage and even loss of life.

BLIZZARDS

Not all bad weather happens in the summer. Just ask someone caught in a blizzard! To be categorized as a blizzard by the National Weather Service, the storm must last at least three hours, produce large amounts of snow, and have winds blowing at a minimum of 35 miles per hour. A ground blizzard meets the same requirement, except that the snow isn't falling down from the atmosphere but instead is whipped up from the ground.

Because of a blizzard's blinding snow, visibility is reduced to one-quarter mile or less. Whiteout conditions are often present during blizzards, with the whirling, blowing snow turning everything white, hiding landmarks, and making it difficult to gauge distance. You can imagine how hard it is to drive—or even walk—in these conditions.

Blizzards occur when polar winds supply cold temperatures and the westerlies provide moisture and warm temperatures. When two such giant fronts meet, cold winter weather often occurs, and sometimes, that winter weather grows into a blizzard.

While extreme weather always poses a threat to humankind and our habitats, we have made great advances in the science and technology of predicting weather so we can move out of its way whenever possible. In the next chapter, we'll take a look at some of the skills meteorologists use when studying the weather.

STAYING SAFE

"Be prepared" should be the motto for all types of extreme weather! For instance, prepare for an oncoming blizzard by stocking extra food and water in your house just in case weather prevents you from leaving home for several days. You should also have a battery-powered radio available, warm clothes, flashlights, candles, and plenty of blankets. If you live in a hurricane area during hurricane season, you should probably have extra gasoline for your car and a bag packed with clothes and your most important possessions in case you have to evacuate.

Depending on where you live, you might face extreme weather. You can't change the weather, but preparation can help you survive it.

KEY QUESTIONS

- **What are the three stages of a thunderstorm?**

- **What is the best course of action when a tornado warning sounds in your area?**

- **Why does a hurricane lose force when it moves over land?**

THUNDERSTORM IN PICTURES

A thunderstorm can be impressive and terrifying at the same time, and understanding its formation is critical to understanding the super-sized storms that sometimes follow. Try to explain the step-by-step development of a supercell storm using drawings and as few words as possible.

- **Look back at how a supercell storm forms.** Find even more detailed descriptions on the internet.

- **On a piece of paper, draw a minimum of eight panels.** This will be your storyboard. Artists and comics use storyboards to plan their plots and drawings before tackling a finished product.

- **In each panel, draw a detailed sketch of a step in the thunderstorm's development.** You can add characters and create a storyline that describes the formation of the storm.

- **Once you are happy with your sketches and the plot, redo the comic strip on new paper and add color.** Share it with friends and classmates to see if they can learn something about how a supercell storm forms.

> **To investigate more,** consider that thunderstorms can be terrifying, but they are also beautiful. People have written poems about storms! Look over your illustrations and written descriptions. Rewrite the steps of the formation of a thunderstorm as accurately as you can—only do it as a poem! Use as many lines as you used panels. Can you attempt some rhyming lines?

Chapter 5 ▶
Weather Watchers

IT'S HUMAN NATURE TO TRY AND PREDICT THE WEATHER.

How has weather watching evolved throughout the ages?

From earliest times until now, people have watched the weather in order to predict it. Each technological advance brought more knowledge, fueled more curiosity, and created more questions, which, of course, led to the next technological advance!

Although the understanding of weather has changed as centuries have passed, the goal has not. People throughout time have watched the weather in order to prepare for, and protect themselves from, whatever lies ahead.

For most of human existence, our understanding of weather has been qualitative.

This means that people studied and learned about weather by observing its qualities. Figuring out that the sun causes heat by observing that at night, or under thick clouds, the heat disappears, is an example of a qualitative understanding of weather. Predicting rain after noticing darkening clouds and a wind kicking up is another example of a qualitative weather forecast. Eventually, though, our growing interest in understanding the world around us demanded quantitative information as well.

We created tools to measure different elements of the weather, and with each tool came a leap in learning. For instance, the invention of the barometer came along with the new understanding that air had weight. The use of images taken by satellites revolutionized our understanding of how weather works on a global basis.

Today, weather forecasting is more important than ever. Take a minute to think about all the businesses that depend on accurate weather forecasts in order to keep humming along.

The Global Precipitation Measurement (GPM) Core Observatory tracks the globe's weather from space.
credit: NASA

Aviation needs up-to-the-minute weather information for plotting out the quickest and safest routes for air travel. Trucking companies also need accurate weather information. Construction companies need daily forecasts to keep their workers safe and their projects moving along on time.

Stores want to know when to bring in extra snow shovels, raincoats, and groceries, while highway workers need to know when to prepare to clear the roads in ice or snowstorms. Sporting events organizers need to know about incoming bad weather to keep their players and fans safe. After extreme weather events, local home improvement stores often ship materials for repair from one part of the country to another.

Weather forecasting is a complex
task because weather is a complex system.

Today's meteorologists need to understand
mathematics, physics, chemistry, computer
programming, and more. Impressed? You should be!
Forecasting the weather is an important job, and
it has become more crucial and more important as
time has gone by. Let's go back and take a look
at the early days of weather forecasting so we can
better understand today's world of meteorology.

EARLY WEATHER FORECASTING

In ancient societies, weather was thought to be
created by the gods in response to human behavior.
Therefore, understanding the weather meant
identifying the behavior most likely to make and
keep the gods happy. The first weather forecasters
were priests or holy men acting as human
intermediaries with the gods. Their job was to help
the members of their community to create rituals
and promote behavior that made the gods content.

For example, the ancient Mayans offered human
sacrifices to keep the gods happy, and therefore
the weather good. Native Americans performed
rain dances. And in Greek mythology, the forces of
nature were explained by personifying elements of
the weather as gods.

Although early human scientific knowledge might
have been lacking, our knowledge of nature was
not. A close relationship with nature yielded a wide
range of information that was used to predict the
weather. This information helped determine when to
set sail and when to stay home, when to plant and
harvest crops, and when to store food for the winter.

In Greek mythology, Zeus was the
god of weather.

As the centuries passed, humans became more advanced in their understanding of the world. In 350 BCE, the Greek philosopher Aristotle (382–322 BCE) gathered together the most important scientific knowledge of the time in his four-volume text titled *Meteorlogica*. He shared theories about the formation of rain clouds, hail, wind, and thunder.

Although many of the ideas were wrong, some of Aristotle's beliefs still hold true today, 2,400 years later! For instance, he believed that the sun put large masses of air into motion (it does) and that water vapor was part of our air (it is).

It wasn't until the Renaissance Period (approximately 1300–1700 CE) that curiosity about the natural world, including the weather, prompted the invention of tools to measure its different elements.

Several of the instruments invented at that time are still in use.

For example, today, we take knowing the temperature for granted. It's pretty easy to glance at a thermometer hanging on a wall or even at a smartphone, if you have a temperature app. Before a version of the thermometer was invented in 1593 based on discoveries made by Galileo Galilei, people's understanding of temperature was purely personal and experiential—they stepped outside to see if it was hot or cold.

Other tools invented during the Renaissance include the first hygrometer, created in the mid-fifteenth century by Nicholas Cusa (1401–1464), a German scientist. The hygrometer measures the amount of humidity in the air. In 1643, Evangelista Torricelli invented the barometer to measure air pressure.

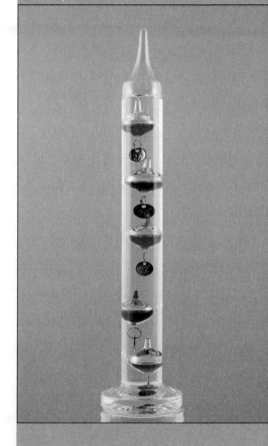

A Galilean thermometer uses bubbles of fluids of different densities floating in a tube of liquid. The bubbles rise or sink depending on the temperatures of the fluids!

Here are Thomas Jefferson's weather observations on July 4, 1776.

6 a.m.   68 degrees
Clear/light north wind

9 a.m.   72 degrees
Mostly sunny

 1 p.m.   76 degrees
Increasing clouds

Read more about Jefferson's weather observations at this website.

Jefferson weather

In the United States, the first systematic weather observations occurred at Swedes' Fort in Delaware in 1644 to 1645. This trend of methodical observation and documentation of weather continued through the 1700s and beyond. Even before he flew his kite in a thunderstorm in 1752, founding father Benjamin Franklin (1706–1790) was observing, analyzing, and documenting the movement of storms and various weather patterns. American statesman and third president of the United States, Thomas Jefferson (1743–1826) recorded the weather daily at his home in Monticello, Virginia—even on July 4, 1776, when he was busy signing the Declaration of Independence!

One of the most important inventions to advance the study of weather was the telegraph in 1843, allowing weather information from all around the country to be shared almost instantaneously.

A climate map from 1823

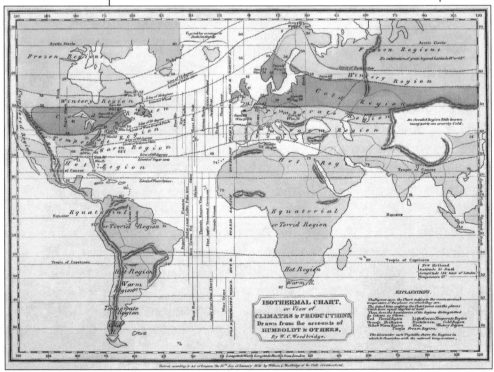

Weather observation stations began popping up all around the globe. The first synoptic weather maps were created by taking many individual bits of weather information from a whole country and putting them together using a visual explanation.

In the mid-1800s, Robert Fitzroy (1805–1865), a British naval officer, began using the gathered information to create weather forecasts. Although others laughed at the absurdity of this idea, Fitzroy wanted to send out weather warnings to ships in order to save lives. By 1861, a London newspaper was publishing a daily weather forecast based on Fitzroy's information.

In the United States, the Weather Bureau (later known as the National Weather Service) joined the forecasting rage in 1870. Forecasts at that time relied solely on basic observation of sky conditions and measurements of air pressure and temperature. Although they were vague, short-term, and lacked much detail, the public loved them. Imagine how it must have felt to get a glimpse of the future!

In 1904, the idea of using mathematical equations to predict the weather was introduced by Vilhelm Bjerknes (1862–1951), a Norwegian scientist. Lewis Fry Richardson (1881–1953), a British mathematician, ran with the idea and developed a strategy between 1913 and 1922.

Although Richardson's work had potential, there was a problem— it took several months of computing by hand to create a single, 24-hour forecast. A little late to be of use!

THE POWER OF THE WEATHER

Have you ever had to change your plans because of the weather? Maybe a baseball game was canceled or you weren't able to go swimming because of thunder and lightning. Imagine that the events affected by the weather were bigger than baseball games and swimming. Imagine that the weather conditions turned the course of a war or destroyed crops in a nation already under stress and sparked a revolution. In the past, when predicting weather was a pretty hit-or-miss practice, it was easy to make mistakes and miscalculations when planning an attack. Even today, weather can affect the outcome of major national and international decisions, such as the decision to go to battle, launch a rocket, or send humanitarian aid. Take a look at some of the past events that might have turned out much differently if the weather had decided to cooperate.

 Livescience weather history

Technology caught up with Richardson's idea in the early 1940s, when two scientists at the University of Pennsylvania began work on ENIAC (Electronic Numerical Integrator and Computer), the world's first general-purpose computer. ENIAC was funded by the U.S. Army, but the war ended before the computer could be used.

However, in 1946, mathematician John von Neumann (1903–1957) was using ENIAC for another purpose when he realized that it could predict weather. Four years later, von Neumann and his team had created the first computer-based numerical weather forecast.[1]

TODAY'S TOOLS

Today's basic meteorological tools are updated versions of previous tools used in new ways. NASA sends thermometers into space via satellite. Barometers record atmospheric pressure changes in an isolated weather station in Antarctica, while an automatic anemometer measures wind speed as it bobs on a buoy in the ocean or is dropped into a hurricane.

You can even get a hygrometer
app for your smartphone!

A primary source of upper-air data is the radiosonde, which is carried aloft by a weather balloon. As the balloon ascends to an altitude exceeding 115,000 feet, the radiosonde measures air pressure, temperature, wind speed, wind direction, and relative humidity, continually sending the data back to earth via radio signals. Eventually the balloon pops and the radiosonde floats back to earth.

If you happen to stumble upon a radiosonde that has landed in your area, this is what you do.

weather.gov radiosonde information

WEATHER WISDOM

About 75,000 radiosondes are sent up in the atmosphere every year from more than 800 upper-air observation stations located around the globe. The observations are taken twice a day at the same time, 365 days a year. During severe weather, a bonus balloon is sent up for additional information.

The radiosonde is built to withstand extremes. During its flight, the radiosonde may experience temperatures as cold as -130 degrees Fahrenheit (-90 degrees Celsius) and air pressure less than 1 percent of the earth's.

During World War II, Navy researchers developed and used radar to detect enemy ships and planes. Today, meteorologists use Doppler radar to locate precipitation and measure its direction and speed. Microwaves are sent out into the atmosphere. When they locate precipitation, they bounce back to the radar dish. The intensity and the return speed of the microwaves tells meteorologists how far away a storm is, its direction and speed, and the amount of precipitation it carries.

Weather is global. Since what happens in one part of the world affects other parts, it makes sense that accurate weather data needs to be gathered from every corner of the globe.

This work is accomplished through many means. More than 900 Automated Surface Observing Systems (ASOS) are located across the United States alone. Using basic instruments for measuring temperature, air pressure, wind speed, and humidity, these stations automatically gather this data and send it back to a central database multiple times a day. In addition, specially outfitted airplanes and ships take measurements and samples. Hundreds of weather buoys, either anchored or adrift, gather information as they float across the oceans of the world.

The National Weather Service has 155 Doppler radar sites gathering information. Learn more about the latest technology and how it works, plus check out some Doppler imagery, at this website.

PS

iweathernet
Doppler radar

Automated Surface Observing System (ASOS) installation

credit: NOAA

A dropsonde is a radiosonde that is dropped out of an airplane over water. It is attached to a parachute and it measures storm conditions along with pressure, temperature, and humidity as it falls. This information is relayed to the airplane by radio. Take a look in this video!

 dropsonde video

Can you guess why the Northern Hemisphere has more ASOS sites than the Southern Hemisphere? If you think it is because the Northern Hemisphere has more land and more people, you are right!

Small, unmanned aircraft called drones are fast becoming an important tool in weather prediction. They operate and gather information in the lower levels of the atmosphere, where most weather takes place. Weather balloons only pass through this layer and it is too low for airplanes to fly safely.

Drones are relatively inexpensive to make and to use, and some of the larger ones can operate for longer than 24 hours.

Finally, satellites are used to track Earth's weather systems. On April 1, 1960, TIROS (Television Infrared Observation Satellite), the very first weather satellite, was carried into space on a rocket. It was 42 inches in diameter and 19 inches high, weighed 270 pounds, and orbited 450 miles above Earth.

Made of aluminum alloy and stainless steel and covered with 9,200 solar cells to charge its onboard batteries, TIROS sent back grainy images of large clouds moving though the atmosphere. Although it operated for only 78 days, TIROS provided thousands of images of Earth's weather, proving that satellites were a valuable tool for studying global weather from space.

TIROS was the first of many satellites sent into space. Currently, the National Oceanic and Atmospheric Administration (NOAA) operates several geostationary satellites and polar orbiting satellites.

TIROS, 1960

credit: NASA

Geostationary Operational Environmental Satellite (GOES) is a system of geostationary satellites. A satellite is typically stationed at a height of 122,300 miles, and it orbits at the same speed that the earth rotates while it monitors one region. Taking pictures in quick succession, it sends the images back to the receiving station, where meteorologists string these pictures together to create movies that allow them to watch the development and movement of storms, fronts, and hurricanes.

Forecasters can also determine wind speed by watching cloud movement. GOES systems monitor severe weather systems, wildfires, lightning, and other weather hazards, so that forecasters can issue watches and warnings when necessary.

The polar orbiting satellites, part of the POES (Polar Operating Environmental Satellite) system, orbit from pole to pole, close to the earth's surface at approximately 520 miles. Because the earth is rotating below it, the polar satellites capture different views of the earth with each of their 14 daily orbits. Their closer proximity to Earth allows them to capture much more detailed information about clouds and weather systems than GOES.[2]

Have you heard of chaos theory? How might it affect weather forecasting? Take a look!

 PS

PBS El Niño predict weather

SUPERCOMPUTERS

Supercomputers are a pivotal part of weather monitoring and predicting. These large and fast computers are especially useful for calculating scientific data. The National Weather Service (NWS) uses supercomputers to collect and organize millions of observations and measurements every day.

Measurements of temperature, air pressure, humidity, and wind speed are plugged into a series of mathematical equations that create weather models up to 16 days in the future. These models predict the formation, intensity, and movement of various weather systems, including how they influence each other and how they are influenced by weather patterns such as the jet stream.

NWS models are used to predict global weather, hurricanes, ocean waves, storm surges, flooding, and even air quality. Based on the models, the NWS creates forecasts as well as watches and warnings that are then sent out to weather stations as well as private businesses.

Without supercomputers, the fast, accurate forecasts we receive today would be impossible!

PREDICTING THE WEATHER

So, if supercomputers gather and analyze the weather data and then create predictions based on that data, how come those weather predictions are sometimes wrong?

Although your day-to-day weather might seem specific to your region or state, it is important to remember that all weather is related. This means that weather happening on the other side of the world right now could affect weather that is happening near you a week from now. And although weather data is being collected from all around the world, the world is a big place. Weather isn't recorded everywhere. A small, insignificant disturbance or cloud or wind storm that isn't recorded in one place could, during several days, grow into a major storm. If the data isn't collected, the computer can't factor it into its model when it computes weather. This leads to incorrect forecasts.

Forecasters correct for this possibility by running two or more related-but-different models, using the same data for both. This creates a set of forecasts that show the range of possibilities for future weather.

A NWS forecast faces one last check—an experienced, trained meteorologist looks at the weather models and decides if they are accurate. While supercomputers are good at analyzing and putting together huge amounts of data in a short time, humans are still an important and necessary part of the process.

WEATHER WISDOM

The combined processing power of the NWS supercomputers is more than 10,000 times faster than the average desktop computer.

As scientist are learning more about severe weather, they are also getting clues that might help them with earlier predictions. Check out some of the science in this video.

predict severe weather NBC

WEATHER-READY NATION

One of NOAA's missions is to help the United States become a weather-ready nation. On its website, NOAA describes that mission this way, "The National Weather Service is committed to ensuring the safety of our citizens and protecting their livelihoods by providing the best observations, forecasts, and warnings, and linking those directly to life-saving decisions made in every community. We are continuously working to improve our forecast and warning capabilities, to better communicate the uncertainty inherent in extended forecasts, and to better connect forecasts and warnings to life and property-saving decisions."[3]

A meteorologist will look at past weather patterns and the weather that is currently happening to see if the forecast makes sense.

It is important to remember that weather predictions will never be 100-percent accurate. But as technology and weather knowledge continue to improve, so will the accuracy of weather forecasting.

PREDICTING SEVERE WEATHER

As weather events increase in intensity and frequency because of climate change, the consequences of severe weather also increase, because more and more people, businesses, cities, and infrastructures are adversely affected by storms. In recent years, scientists have put a lot of effort into researching severe weather in order to improve forecasting, since time is a crucial factor when people are preparing an area for a severe storm. Evacuations, property protection, and stocking up on necessities all require advanced warning.

What's causing weather events to become more extreme? Climate change is a big part of the answer. In the next chapters, we'll take a look at the climate and how it fluctuates, and explore the connection between climate change and extreme weather.

KEY QUESTIONS

- **What is the difference between qualitative and quantitative ways of obtaining weather information? Which is more useful for making accurate predictions?**
- **What is a weather model and how does it work?**
- **Why is accurate and timely weather forecasting more important than ever?**

WATCHING WEATHER UNFOLD

As you've read, the weather that happened yesterday or the day before that affects the weather you are experiencing today. Take some time to actually see what that flow of weather from one place to another looks like.

- **Each day, for five days in a row, collect a weather map from the same source.** It would be best if the map covered a large area, such as the whole United States. Make sure you write the date on all your maps. Check out this article for tips on how to read a weather map.

   scijinks
  weather map

- **After five days, spread out the maps chronologically.** Record your observations of the weather in your science journal. Which way did the fronts move? How long did a high- or low-pressure system stay in an area? Did any landforms affect the movement of weather systems? How did the temperatures change in a single area?

- **Now is your chance to see the weather unfold.** What do you notice about the maps in relation to your own observations?

> **To investigate more,** use the information gained from studying the last five days of weather to create your own forecast and synoptic map for the sixth day. Where will the fronts and pressure systems move next? How will the temperatures change? Will there be new weather coming in?

VOCAB LAB

Write down what you think each word means. What root words can you find to help you? What does the context of the word tell you?

geostationary, hygrometer, qualitative, quantitative, and **radar**.

Compare your definitions with those of your friends or classmates. Did you all come up with the same meanings? Turn to the text and glossary if you need help.

WATCHING THE WEATHER

Weather forecasts have become an important and sizeable part of each day's daily, local television news. But as you've been learning, weather is a complex, global system. Now is your chance to apply some of the information that you learned.

- **With your science journal in hand, watch a weather forecast online.** You can pause it to take notes and replay parts that you want to hear again.

- **When it is done, jot down your answers to the following questions.**

  - Did you understand the terms the weather person used?

  - Did you understand the reasons behind the movement of weather?

  - Did the forecast provide too much information or not enough?

  - Did the personality of the weather person play a part in the forecast? If so, was that a help or a hindrance to your understanding of the information you were getting?

  - Did a knowledge of the science behind how and why weather happens help your interest in and understanding of the forecast?

- **Do you have any other reflections or questions?** Write them down as well.

To investigate more, read this article about the life and job of a meteorologist.

 scijinks meteorologist

Do you have any interest in pursuing a career in meteorology? What strengths or skills do you have that might make this career a good one for you?

Chapter 6 ▶
The Science of Climate

UNDERSTANDING HOW WE CHANGE OUR CLIMATE IS VERY IMPORTANT TO OUR EARTH'S HEALTH!

Why is it important to understand past and present climates?

We can't take care of and protect our Earth unless we understand it. To understand climate change, scientists must first understand climate, which means studying climate patterns of the past and recognizing the ways those patterns are changing today.

A friend is thinking of moving to your area and asks you to describe it. How would you do that? What would you say? You would probably mention the predominant weather where you live—not the daily weather, but general weather patterns. If you have seasons, you'd probably describe the weather patterns associated with those. You might talk about the kind of outdoor recreation your area has to offer and describe some of the natural beauty.

Weather patterns, seasons, outdoor recreation, and ecosystems—in other words, much of your answer would have to do, either directly or indirectly, with the climate of your area!

How does the climate of your area affect your daily life? Your region's climate dictates its agriculture, and, maybe, its food preferences. Tourism is often related to climate. People do not travel to Florida to ski, unless they plan to do it on water!

Many businesses, such as hotels, restaurants, and stores, depend on climate-based recreation. Beach shoes aren't sold in Montana in winter and Southern California stores don't stock long underwear for chilly winter days.

Local infrastructure is built with climate in mind, as are buildings, large and small. For instance, a downtown area in a coastal region might be surrounded by a seawall, while roofs in snowy areas need to be engineered to hold the weight of heavy snow.

In the same way that weather predictions help businesses and city governments make daily decisions, climate predictions help them make long-term decisions. As climates change, city planners and businesses must accommodate those changes.

> The flooding that can follow superstorms or higher temperatures in mountain areas that depend on winter snow for tourism are both examples of how changes in climate can affect towns and cities.

Plus, climate is very closely tied to the ecosystem of an area. Ecosystems are held together and kept in balance by the climate of the area. If one thing changes in that web of life, everything else in that web is affected.

Just as an understanding of how the human body functions is essential to staying healthy, an understanding of Earth's climates, of where and how they affect our lives, gives us the necessary knowledge to maintain our planet's health. And arming yourself with an understanding of climate will help you to correctly evaluate the scientific information coming out regarding climate change.

WEATHER WISDOM

The fewest species of plants and animals are found where conditions are the harshest, such as the Arctic. The most varieties are found in warm, wet tropical areas. The areas where the margins of survival are the narrowest are also the most vulnerable to small changes in the climate.

Polar bears are just one species that has been adversely affected by climate change. They need the ice to hunt, but because their habitats have less ice now, these animals are struggling to get enough food to survive.

credit: Mario Hoppmann, NASA Goddard Space Flight Center

FACTORS INFLUENCING CLIMATE

Climate is the average pattern of weather occurring in a region during a time span of many years. The oceans, landforms, atmosphere, plants and animals, and energy of the sun all work together to create Earth's wide variety of regional climates.

In contrast, the global climate is the climate of our entire planet. The global climate is described by the average temperature of the earth's surface.

Latitude is one of the main factors that determines a region's climate. In general, the closer an area is to the equator, the more direct sunlight it gets, and therefore the hotter it is. Conversely, the closer an area is to the poles, the less direct sunlight it gets, and the colder it is.

How long has the earth been around? Here's a quick look at the geological time scale.

geological time scale

Generally, seasonal variations are also due to latitude. Midlatitude regions have four distinct seasons, while areas close to the equator or the poles generally only have two. Altitude also affects climate because the higher the altitude, the cooler the temperatures.

Proximity to large bodies of water affects a region's temperature and humidity. Water holds heat longer and gives it off more slowly than land. So, regions next to large bodies of water have temperatures that fluctuate less than regions that are landlocked. Coastal regions tend to be cooler than landlocked regions in the summer and warmer than landlocked regions in the winter.

Large areas of ice affect temperature and therefore climate because they act as giant mirrors, reflecting the heat of the sun instead of absorbing it. Landforms, such as a mountain range, can also affect the climate of a region by consistently blocking wind and precipitation. So, when a storm traveling east from the Pacific Ocean hits the Rocky Mountains, the precipitation-carrying clouds are blocked or emptied out on the windward side, creating a drier climate on the leeward, or far side, of the mountain.

Global winds and ocean currents also play their part in world climates. As they circulate predictably throughout the planet, they constantly bring warm air to cold regions and cool air to warm regions.

CLIMATE WISE

Humans have learned to adapt to almost every climate. They do this not by adding on a layer of blubber to keep them warm, as the polar bear does, or by sprouting prickly spines, such as the desert cactus. Humans adapt through the things they make, including clothing and homes. People who live in the north wear thick coats that allow them to go outside even when the temperature is well below freezing. Sunblock and skin-covering clothing mean humans can spend time outdoors with less fear of sunburn or skin cancer, even in places where the sun shines hot and long. What other technologies have we created to allow us to adapt to all kinds of climates?

In this image of the Himalayan Mountains, you can see on which side of the mountain range the rain usually falls.

CLIMATE ZONES

Scientists use a variety of classification systems to define and describe the world's climates. One frequently used system is the Köppen climate classification system, proposed by Wladimir Köppen (1846–1940), a Russian-German climatologist and botanist, in 1900. Köppen's classification is based on the native vegetation, the temperature, and precipitation of an area. According to the Köppen system, there are five climate groups, starting at the equator and spreading out toward the poles.

Although Köppen identified these climate groups with a capital letter, they are also referred to by a name that describes the general temperature and humidity: Tropical (A), Dry (B), Temperate (C), Continental (D) and Polar (E). These large-scale classifications are further divided into subgroups to reflect the smaller-scale differences found in regions.

Check out Köppen's climate map with categories and subcategories. Which region do you live in?

 World Map KöppenGeiger

Köppen Classification

Climate Zone Name	Latitude	Description	Example of City in Zone
(A) Tropical	Equator to 15–25 degrees north and south	Warm and humid. All months have average temperature above 64 degrees Fahrenheit (18 degrees Celsius) and annual precipitation of 59 inches.	Manaus, Brazil
(B) Dry	20 degrees to 35 degrees north and south	Evaporation exceeds precipitation. Also found in midlatitude areas surrounded by mountains.	Cairo, Egypt
(C) Continental/Mild	30 degrees to 50 degrees north and south	Warm, humid summers and mild winters. Found on eastern and western borders of most continents. Thunderstorms in summer.	Madrid, Spain
(D) Continental/Cold	50 degrees north and south and toward the poles	Average temperature of warmest month is above 50 degrees Fahrenheit (10 degrees Celsius) while the coldest month temperature is below -22 degrees Fahrenheit (-30 degrees Celsius). Winters are severe and bitter cold.	Bratsk, Russia
(E) Polar	North and South Poles	Cold temperatures year round with warmest month's temperatures below 50 degrees Fahrenheit (10 degrees Celsius).	Barrow, Alaska

CHANGE AND SCIENCE

Climatologists use many of the same tools as meteorologists, including satellites and weather stations, to measure atmosphere, temperature, cloud cover, snow pack, and glacier size. Comparing current data to that of past years helps climatologists understand past climates and might make it possible to determine climate trends in the future.

> The earth's climate is always changing, going from warmer to colder periods and back again.

Most changes happen during an extended span of time, allowing animals and people and plants to adapt. For instance, 600 million years ago, our earth was covered with snow and thick ice, stretching from the poles to the equator. And 120 million years ago, dinosaurs roamed the earth and volcanoes spewed greenhouse gases into the atmosphere, creating areas of hot, humid rainforest. The final ice age lasted until 12,000 years ago.[1]

You might be wondering how scientists know about the earth's long-ago climactic changes, without any written records or photos of what life on Earth was like then! The answer is paleoclimatology, the study of Earth's past climates. Although scientists cannot directly study climactic conditions of the past, they can "read" Earth's climate history by collecting information left from ancient climates.

Take a quick visit to Antarctica, where the ice sheet is between 1 and 4 miles thick! How is life in that climate different from where you live? How do people need to adapt to survive in extreme cold? What about extreme heat?

 Lonely Planet Antarctica

Bubbles trapped in Antarctic ice
credit: CSIRO (CC BY 3.0)

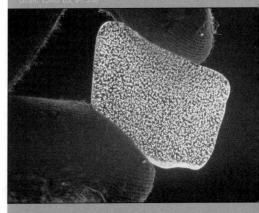

An ice core sample from Greenland

credit: Fred W. Baker III, U.S. Department of Defense

This indirect data, called proxy data, is obtained from multiple sources that are pieced together and compared to current knowledge. As paleoclimatologists study these remnants of a long-ago climate, they can work out a timeline of the earth's past.

Ice core sampling is one way of obtaining proxy data. Ancient ice sheets and glaciers formed as winter snow fell and didn't melt. This process repeated itself for thousands of years, trapping dust and gas molecules. Today, scientists can remove a narrow cylinder of ice from the ice fields in the Antarctic or Greenland and analyze the air bubbles trapped inside. It helps them to learn about the composition of the atmosphere from the time the air was trapped.

The oldest ice core sample is from ice formed 800,000 years ago!

Learn more about how ice core samples are taken and studied in this video.

 Maine ice core

We can also study sample cores taken from the ocean's floor. Just as snow piled up on land, layer upon layer of dust, dirt, and plant and animal remains piled up at the bottom of the ocean. The sediment samples from the ocean floors can reveal 170 million years of history!

Scientists know that the more plant and animal biodiversity found in a layer, the more hospitable the environment was when it was formed. Also, the types of fossilized plants and animals in the sample give information about the type of weather that was happening at the time the sediment was formed.

Landscapes give scientists a
view into past climates.

Valleys carved out by glaciers leave evidence of where and when the ice ages took place. One rock layer laid bare by erosion might show volcanic ash, while another layer might reveal the signs of an ancient, inland sea.

Have you ever counted the rings of a tree that's been cut down? You probably know that the width of tree rings inside a trunk show their yearly growth. Wide rings mean that the climate was conducive to good growth, whereas narrow or nonexistent rings might mean drought.

TODAY'S CLIMATE CHANGE

Today, the earth is experiencing a warming of temperatures that can't be attributed to natural causes. Scientists have been monitoring the earth's temperatures and collecting reliable data for the last 100 years—based on that information, we know that this warming is due at least in part to humans' use of fossil fuels, such as coal, oil, and gas.

Fossil fuels account for most of the energy that the world's population uses today. As the population of the planet increases, and our technology creates more and more tools and mechanisms that require energy to power them, the use of fossil fuels seems to have no end in sight.

In Chapter 7, we'll take a peak at the future of our climate.

VOCAB LAB

Write down what you think each word means. What root words can you find to help you? What does the context of the word tell you?

biodiversity, ecosystem, latitude, paleoclimatology, and **windward.**

Compare your definitions with those of your friends or classmates. Did you all come up with the same meanings? Turn to the text and glossary if you need help.

KEY QUESTIONS

- **How does the climate of your area affect your daily life?**

- **Have you noticed anything about the climate that has changed in your lifetime?**

- **What are some things you already do to help protect the planet?**

Ideas for Supplies ▼

- blank world map with latitude labeled
- charts of Köppen classification zones:

 world map latitude print

CLIMATE ZONE MAP

Most of us know the basics of our own climate through day-to-day experience. But how much do you really know about the various climate regions of the world? Let's put weather events in context around the world.

- **Use a world map and the classification chart on page 88.** Color and label each of the five general climate zones on the world map.

- **Do some research!** Using the internet or books from your local library, research each of the climate zones. Look for information that helps you picture and understand each region more fully. Collect descriptive words, interesting climate facts, and images of landscapes, plants, and animals. Identify countries and cities or well-known destinations located in each zone.

- **When you feel as though you have a clear sense of each of the five main regions,** create a poster to accompany your map.

> **To investigate more,** combine some of your previous learning from this book with your new knowledge of the five major climate zones. On your climate zone map, label or make note of the location of the major air masses. Add the global wind and ocean currents. How do the elements of the world's weather affect each of the climates? Write down your thoughts in your science journal.

Chapter 7 ▶
Our Changing Climate

YOU CAN BATTLE CLIMATE CHANGE BY PAYING ATTENTION TO YOUR ENVIRONMENTAL FOOTPRINT!

What can people do to be a part of the solution to the problem of climate change?

SO, CUTTING DOWN ON SINGLE-USE ITEMS HELPS OUR CLIMATE?

YES!

SINGLE-USE ITEMS USE UP LOTS OF ENERGY TO MAKE, PACKAGE, AND TRANSPORT.

SO, WE NEED TO STOP BUYING SINGLE-USE ITEMS AND GO THE REUSABLE ROUTE TO REDUCE OUR CARBON FOOTPRINT.

YES! REDUCING AND REUSING HELP COMBAT CLIMATE CHANGE. RECYCLING SHOULD BE A LAST RESORT.

While governments and businesses must make strides to reduce their reliance on energy from nonrenewable resources, individuals can take plenty of steps as well. Only by working together can humans rescue the planet we know and rely on!

It's dinner time. You're hungry and want something quick and easy to eat, so your family drives a gasoline-powered car to the 24-hour grocery store. Thanks to electricity, the store is warm and toasty, its lights are blazing, the cash register is clicking, and the refrigerator case is humming.

Roaming through the aisles, you see an abundance of food items, all of which were delivered by a diesel-powered truck and, before that, a diesel- or electric-powered train, from a warehouse heated and lit by electricity. Most of the processed food that you are looking at is packaged in layers of plastic and cardboard, all of which were manufactured in factories that required electricity to run.

The food itself, also processed in a factory, was made from individual ingredients that were shipped from separate factories.

For instance, wheat was planted, grown, and harvested using farm equipment powered by gasoline or diesel fuel. It was then driven to a plant to be ground into flour. The flour was driven to another plant and used in a recipe with other ingredients, packaged in plastic and cardboard, driven to a warehouse, and then driven to the store, where the meal is now sitting on a shelf waiting for you to buy it.

Which you do! After driving home, you zap your dinner in the microwave and sit down to a quick and easy meal.

The above scenario is repeated millions of times by millions of people every minute of the day. Our daily lives take lots and lots of energy. And most of that energy comes from fossil fuels. It powers our homes, our cars, our electronics. And, unfortunately, we now know that fossil fuels also power climate change. Let's take a look at how.

But first, let's make sure we have our terms straight. Global warming refers to the increase of the earth's average temperature through time, while modern climate change refers to all the changes to our climate brought about through global warming. In this book, both terms are used to refer to changes brought about by human activity.[1]

GREENHOUSE GASES

The Earth's atmosphere is made up of 78 percent nitrogen and 21 percent oxygen. The remaining 1 percent includes carbon dioxide, methane, nitrous oxide, water vapor, and ozone, also known as greenhouse gases. Although just a tiny part of our atmosphere, greenhouse gases play a big role in our climate. Here's how.

The greater the population, the more of Earth's resources are being used. But not all people, and not all countries, consume those resources equally. Although people in the United States make up only 5 percent of the world's population, they use 21 percent of the world's energy.

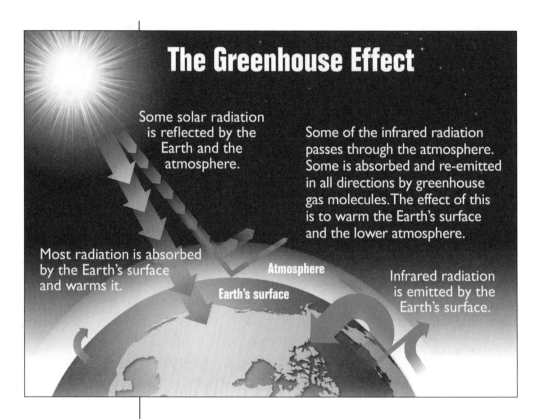

The Greenhouse Effect

Some solar radiation is reflected by the Earth and the atmosphere.

Some of the infrared radiation passes through the atmosphere. Some is absorbed and re-emitted in all directions by greenhouse gas molecules. The effect of this is to warm the Earth's surface and the lower atmosphere.

Most radiation is absorbed by the Earth's surface and warms it.

Atmosphere

Earth's surface

Infrared radiation is emitted by the Earth's surface.

For a more in-depth explanation of greenhouse gases, check out this video.

 UCAR Scott Denning

When the sun's heat enters our atmosphere, it is absorbed by the earth's surface. Some of it is then radiated back into space. Greenhouse gases trap some of that heat before it escapes back into space, radiating it back to the earth's surface. This is known as the greenhouse effect. Without greenhouse gases, the earth's average temperature would be 0.4 degrees Fahrenheit (-18 degrees Celsius), too cold to sustain most life. For most of human existence on Earth, greenhouse gases kept our atmosphere just right.

And then, they didn't!

Scientists around the world now agree that the temperature rise, or global warming, that we've seen during the last 150 to 200 years is linked to an increased amount of greenhouse gases in the atmosphere.

But where did all this greenhouse gas come from? The answer is simple: human activity.

TOO MUCH GREENHOUSE GAS

Before the late 1700s, most people lived in agriculture-based communities. They grew most of their food and their few possessions were made by hand or with the use of simple machines. Not much energy was required or consumed.

The Industrial Revolution ushered in massive changes in the late 1700s and early 1800s. During this time, machines were invented to mass-produce common products that up until then were handmade, such as material for clothing. Run by coal-powered steam engines, these machines changed lives. Factories sprouted up all around the United States and people moved to the cities to work in them. Steamships and railroads gave people more mobility. The internal combustion engine was invented in the late 1800s. In 1908, Henry Ford (1863–1947) designed the Model T car and built factories to mass-produce these cars. The world began to move faster.

Progress brought by the Industrial Revolution made life easier, but it was powered by fossil fuels such as coal, oil, and natural gas. From then on, the amount of greenhouse gases, primarily carbon dioxide, dramatically increased in our atmosphere.

According to NASA, the levels of carbon dioxide in the air are currently at their highest in 650,000 years. The global temperature has increased 1.8 degrees Fahrenheit since 1880, with 17 of the 18 warmest years on record occurring since 2001.[2]

What inventions came about because of the Industrial Revolution? Let's take a look in this video.

History Industrial Revolution video

FOSSIL FUELS

We know that fossil fuels are very useful to humans, and we also know that there is a finite amount of them. But how do fossil fuels form? Can we make more? It's a bit complicated. Millions of years ago, tiny plants and animals lived in the ocean. When they died, they sank to the ocean floor and were buried by layers of sand, rock, and mud. Eventually, after millions of years, the weight and pressure of those layers transformed those partially decomposed plants and animals into oil and natural gas. Coal, another fossil fuel, is formed much the same way, except the dead material was tree and plant material that sank to the bottom of swamps and bogs.

HARNESSING METHANE

As organic matter decomposes in landfills, methane is normally vented out into the atmosphere. According to the EPA, landfills are the third largest source of methane emissions in the United States. However, many landfills are now capturing the methane before it reaches the air and routing it to a plant that can use that methane to produce heat or electricity. More and more landfills worldwide are producing this type of energy. In 2009, Germany produced enough electricity this way to power 3.5 million homes.[3]

WEATHER WISDOM

Cars and trucks add a lot of carbon dioxide to the atmosphere, but deforestation is just as bad. According to the World Carfree Network, cars and trucks account for about 14 percent of global carbon emissions, while most analysts attribute upwards of 15 percent to deforestation.

OTHER SOURCES

Aside from overuse of fossil fuels, deforestation is another major cause of global warming. Tropical rainforests are an important part of the global ecosystem, helping to keep the earth in balance. During photosynthesis, trees and plants absorb carbon dioxide from the atmosphere and release oxygen back into it.

Unfortunately, large areas of rainforests have been cut or burned in order to clear the area for farming and grazing. This is bad news for the atmosphere. Losing forests means losing a large supplier of oxygen as well as an important means of cleaning the air. In addition, the cut forests are often replaced by businesses that create more greenhouse gases and hurt the environment.

Large-scale industrial farming is one such business. Plowed fields absorb the sun's energy instead of reflecting it as forests do.

Deforestation in Borneo to make space for a coal mine, 2013

credit: IndoMet in the Heart of Borneo (CC BY 2.0)

Are you a meat eater? Most people are cutting into steak or chicken at some point during the week. As beef has become more and more popular, large-scale ranches are replacing rainforests. Cattle ranches add dangerous amounts of methane, another greenhouse gas that is even more powerful than carbon dioxide. The problem is, cows produce a lot of methane gas as they digest their food, releasing up to 98,420,000 tons of toxic methane gas worldwide.

Another way methane is released into the atmosphere is through garbage dumps and landfills. In many landfills across the world, garbage is covered with dirt and compacted. Without oxygen, the normal decaying process is prevented. Instead, bacteria that do not require oxygen break down the organic remains, producing methane gas that is released into the air.

PREDICTING CLIMATE CHANGE

How do we know how climate change will affect life in the future? Just as scientists create numerical models to predict weather, they use climate models to predict the changes brought on by global warming. Extensive data is constantly collected on surface temperatures, ocean currents, cloud formation, plant cover, and the amount of greenhouse gases in the atmosphere.

To make climate change predictions, scientists change different variables in their models. For example, they ask the question, "How would the climate be affected if there was more cloud cover or fewer forests or warmer ocean temperatures?" And then they look at the results for each variable or combinations of variables.

Methane is 28 times more efficient at trapping the earth's heat than carbon dioxide. In addition, the level of methane in our atmosphere is now higher than at any point in the last 2,000 years.

WEATHER WISDOM

A methane molecule will stay in the air for nine years, while a carbon dioxide molecule stays in the air for 100 years. Therefore, cutting methane emissions through changes in farming, eating habits, and garbage disposal and management could make a big difference fast.

Meet Jessica Hellman, a scientist researching and studying climate change. In her interview, she says, "Always strive to do work that betters humanity and the earth." What kind of work would that mean to you?

LiveScience
Jessica Hellman

Easton Glacier on Mount Baker in the North Cascades of Washington, 2003. You can see how much ice has melted since 1985.

Obviously, this work is extremely complex, because, as you already know, when one thing changes in Earth's climate system, everything is affected. Climate scientists are hard at work piecing together this ever-changing puzzle, constantly gaining and applying new information and insights to the global problem of climate change.

EFFECTS OF GLOBAL WARMING

It is important to note that even if greenhouse gas emissions were completely stopped today, we would continue to see the effects of the gases that are currently in the atmosphere for years to come. Greenhouse gases leave the atmosphere very slowly.

Scientists predict that temperatures will continue to rise, with more warming occurring in the twenty-first century than during the twentieth century. The planet's average surface temperature has risen about 1.8 degrees Fahrenheit since the late 1800s, with most of that warming occurring in the past 35 years.

Although warming temperatures will impact regions differently, the greater increases are expected to be seen over land rather than the ocean. Because of their sensitivity to change, the higher latitudes may see greater changes than the tropics or midlatitudes.

Due to higher temperatures, snow and ice are beginning to melt and glaciers are retreating. Data collected by NASA from 1993 through 2016 shows that the Greenland ice sheet lost an average of 287 billion tons of ice per year, while the Antarctica ice sheet lost 119 billion tons.

> Some researchers predict that before mid-century, the Arctic Ocean will become ice-free during the summers.[4]

As global temperatures rise, water will evaporate at a higher rate, leading to higher levels of precipitation. Again, this will vary according to region, with some locations receiving more rain or snow and others receiving less.

Up until now, the oceans have absorbed much of the increased heat. However, scientists worry that the increased heat, as well as differences in salt content due to the melting of sea ice, may disrupt the global ocean currents, which, as we saw in Chapter 3, are very important in balancing hot and cold temperatures around the world. Ocean currents directly affect the climate of land areas they pass. For example, the coast off the north of England is warmer than inland cities at the same latitude. If those ocean currents change, the climate of the land they pass will also change.

The warmer ocean waters are also thought to contribute to hurricanes of greater intensity and duration. We saw how a hurricane gets its energy from warmer air above the ocean and how it loses energy as it moves over land or over cooler regions of the ocean. If oceans have greater expanses of warm water where hurricanes linger, we could see storms that break records in terms of how long they last and how much damage they do.

WEATHER WISDOM

Scientists estimate that the world has lost one half of its coral reefs in the last 30 years. This loss will have devastating effects because, although they take up only 0.1 percent of the seabed, they support 25 percent of marine life.

Take a look at this interactive website that shows the history of different aspects of climate change.

 NASA climate time machine

Ocean levels throughout the world will continue to rise, as well. They have already risen by about 8 inches since 1880, but are projected to rise another 1 to 4 feet by 2100, depending on the increase or decrease of carbon dioxide in the atmosphere. Do you live near the coast? Millions of people live in coastal areas, where storm surges and high tides will increase flooding—some coastal land areas will even disappear. Since ocean waters take a long time to respond to warming conditions, we will continue to see rising sea levels for many centuries, even as we slow the changing global climate.

What does all of this mean for the plants and animals that share our planet? Climate change affects all ecosystems. As some habitats shrink due to changing temperatures, animals will either move or adapt. Because the time period during which these changes are occurring is short, adaptation is doubtful. It can take many centuries for adaptation to take place. Scientists estimate that many species of plants and animals will be lost in the near future.

Glaciers on retreat in the Bhutan-Himalaya, leaving behind glacial lakes as the ice melts

As habitats are lost and the plant and animal life that they support are also lost, whole ecosystems are destroyed. It's similar to a row of dominoes. For example, coral reefs are part of a complex ecosystem that provides food and shelter for a large variety of fish and other species, such as shrimp, crab, sponges, and starfish.

When the coral reefs die, their loss impacts all the other living things that depend on them for existence, including humans. Coral reefs are a big draw for tourism—so when they die, those industries that depend on tourism die as well. In addition, because coral reefs support so much sea life, many people who live nearby are dependent on them for fishing income and food. Finally, the location of coral reefs protects coastal communities from powerful waves, flooding, and coastal erosion.

> If the coral reefs are destroyed, life in those regions will be vastly different.

Changing weather patterns will also affect the availability of water. The western United States already has less snow accumulation. This is important because the snowpack in the mountains serves as water storage for arid regions. Less snow in winter months means less water available the rest of the year. Eventually, drought, water shortages, and food shortages may result.

Learn about renewable energy sources and talk to your family about exploring the options of at least partially using renewable energy for your own house. Many cities in the country are striving to reduce their carbon emissions. Check and see if your city is one of them. Thinking about shrinking your carbon footprint helps you be aware of your actions in relationship to the world and climate change.

WEATHER WISDOM

There is some good news regarding fossil fuel usage. The U.S. Energy Information Administration (EIA) reports that in 2018, the total U.S. coal consumption was at its lowest level since 1979. This decline is due to both the closing of coal-fired plants and competition from natural gas and renewable sources.

Want to learn some cool facts about renewable energy? Check out this website!

 NASA interesting energy

RENEWABLE SOURCES

Biomass can be burned directly to produce heat, or it can be converted into gas, for example when we capture methane from landfills. Biomass can also be converted to a liquid form, such as the ethanol used to power cars. Geothermal energy is generated by the heat and steam found deep within the earth. Hydropower comes from moving water, wind energy from wind, and solar energy is generated by the sun.

CLEAN ENERGY

Now that you've got the picture of how the world is changing due to climate change, let's think about what we can do to stop it, or at least slow it way down. One major way to combat climate change is to reduce, or eliminate, our dependence on fossil fuels and switch over to clean, renewable energy.

Fossil fuels were created during millions of years, as marine creatures decayed under immense heat and pressure. Once these energy sources are gone, there's no replacing them. In addition to the negative effects of burning fossil fuels, there is also the environmental cost of mining. Pollution, destruction of ecosystems, and tainted water supplies are just a few of those costs. Finally, mining is often dangerous and unhealthy work.

Switching over to renewable energy has many benefits.

First of all, renewable energy is just that, renewable. It won't run out because it comes from sources we already have in abundance. As technology improves, renewable energy continues to become more accessible and affordable, and therefore, a more practical alternative.

The most common forms of renewable energy are solar, wind, hydropower, geothermal, and biomass. The first four energies are considered clean because they don't put greenhouse gases directly into the air.

Although they may create some greenhouse gases through the building and management of their associated equipment, such as solar panels and wind turbines, the amount put into the atmosphere is significantly less. Finally, once built, renewable energy facilities are not costly to run and their energy sources are free. The sun isn't charging!

Of course, there are challenges to widespread renewable energy use. For one, it is difficult for these energies to generate power on the same large scale as fossil fuel companies do. Also, wind and solar power are intermittent—no energy is generated when the wind stops blowing or the sun goes down. And although the energy that is generated can be stored in batteries, often the means of storage is expensive.

Regardless of the downsides, renewable energy is a fast-growing alternative to fossil fuel use. It is being embraced by cities and countries worldwide.

FIGHTING CLIMATE CHANGE

Scientists agree that the best approach to solving the problem of climate change is with a combination of adaptation and mitigation strategies. Adaptation occurs when steps are taken to respond to the environmental changes brought on by climate change, while mitigation is actively working to reduce or eliminate the problems causing it in the first place.

Adaptation includes building sea walls and changing land usage where flooding is due to occur. For instance, the port city of Rotterdam in the Netherlands developed floating neighborhoods that can rise as the oceans rise. The city of Taipei in Taiwan fixed leaks in the water system and saved 613,000 tons of water when faced with increased drought worsened by climate change.

INTERNATIONAL EFFORTS

The United Nations's Paris Climate Accord is an international agreement about the goals needed to mitigate the worst effects of climate change. This agreement, initially signed by 195 nations worldwide, was reached in December 2015 and is aimed at reducing carbon emissions and slowing the rise of global temperatures. The final agreement was signed by 174 nations, including the United States, in 2016. These countries pledged to work to keep the rise of global temperature below 3.6 degrees Fahrenheit (2 degrees Celsius) and, if possible, below 2.7 degrees Fahrenheit (1.5 degrees Celsius). Currently, work is progressing and change is happening. President Donald Trump pulled the United States out of the Paris climate agreement in June 2017, citing a disbelief in the science of climate change as well as the belief that following the guidelines for carbon emissions hurts the economy. However, many American businesses and local governments have continued to honor the guidelines set in the agreement.

Examples of mitigation include Canada ending its coal operations in 2014. China is the world's largest investor in domestic solar energy and Sweden is requiring that the government cut all greenhouse gas emissions by 2045.

WHAT YOU CAN DO

"But I'm just a kid, what can I do?" you might be thinking. Actually, you can do a lot. Remember, big change often starts with small steps.

One of the main ways that you can start being part of the solution to climate change is to reduce your carbon footprint, which is the sum of all emissions of CO_2 indirectly or directly created by your activities in a given timeframe, usually a year. In other words, when you take a trip in a car, the engine fuel creates a certain amount of CO_2 depending on how far you drive. It makes a difference if your car is fuel-efficient and if you carpool or ride the bus. Could you sometimes walk or ride your bike to a friend's house or to school instead of going by car?

Is your house heated with fossil fuels or renewable energy, such as wind or solar?

As of 2017, the breakdown of U.S. energy use looks like this.

EIA energy source

When you buy fruit from the store, is it locally grown or does it come from another country, thereby adding the carbon emissions required to ship it a great distance? Are the products you buy wrapped individually in layers of plastic or can you buy them in larger containers with less wrapping or, better yet, in recyclable containers?

These are just a few of the questions to ask yourself as you begin to pay attention to the environmental footprint you are leaving with almost every single decision that you make throughout the day.

Another easy change to make is to get your family to start buying energy-efficient lightbulbs for household use. LED lights use 75-percent less energy than the old-fashioned incandescent lighting. And, because they last 25 times longer, they are a more economical choice as well.

Energy.gov tells us that if the United States switched entirely to LED lights during the next 20 years, we could save $250 billion, yes, *billion*, in energy costs and reduce the electricity used for lighting by nearly 50 percent. This change alone would avoid 1,800 million metric tons of carbon emissions.[5]

Do you generally use items that can be used only once? If so, now is a great time to make a change. Plastic bags are a single-use item and are not recyclable, so they will stay in a landfill for thousands of years. Being carbon-friendly means replacing plastic bags with reusable grocery bags. And in your lunch, you can switch out individually wrapped packaging with reusable containers.

REDUCE YOUR CARBON FOOTPRINT

Using fossil fuels adds carbon dioxide into the atmosphere. Your carbon footprint is the total of how much carbon dioxide is released into the air because of your energy usage. This includes transportation, electricity, heating and cooling for your house, and even what you purchase. Go back and read this chapter's introduction to see how just one trip to the store adds to your personal carbon footprint. Think about how much you drive, how your house is heated, how much electricity you consume. Find an internet carbon calculator for kids. Fill out the questions on the carbon calculator. How did you do? In your science journal, write down some concrete steps that you could take to reduce your carbon footprint. Do the same thing for your whole family. How is your family doing? Is there anything you could do to reduce your carbon footprint?

There are several calculators to choose from, but here is one that you could take a look at.

 zerofootprint youth

It is also much more energy efficient to use a refillable container for water rather than buying water in single-use plastic bottles.

Eating foods that are in-season and grown locally helps reduce your carbon footprint, as does reducing the amount of meat that you eat.

Finally, scientists warn that another result of global warming and climate change is an increase in extreme weather events, such as extended debilitating heat waves. According to the National Climate Assessment, heat-related illnesses cause more deaths each year than any other type of severe weather.

Another type of weather event brought on by climate change is heavy rain and the resulting floods. In the spring of 2019, the central United States experienced long-lasting rain events that caused catastrophic floods, resulting in the destruction of property and crops. More severe hurricanes, more frequent tornados, less snowfall—these extreme weather events are becoming the new normal, greatly impacting the economy and human health of the areas affected.[6]

Climate change is a story of fast-moving change that is picking up speed as time goes on. This change is seen in Earth's increasing temperatures, in the oceans, and in the bare ground left behind by melting polar ice and receding mountain glaciers. It is also seen in vanishing ecosystems and changes to our atmosphere.

What will be the end of this story? It is up to all of us to decide.

Excited to make a change but don't know where to begin? Read about other kids and what they are doing to help our environment.

roots shoots

KEY QUESTIONS

- **What are some of the factors that are causing climate change? How do your own daily habits contribute to climate change?**

- **How can you reduce your carbon footprint?**

Inquire & Investigate

MELTING ICE

Which has a greater affect on rising levels of the ocean, the melting of ice that is already in the water or ice melting on the land and running off into the water? Here is your chance to find out. You'll need ice, two identical shallow glass containers, and a jar with a lid on it and weights in the bottom so it doesn't float.

- **Measure out two equal amounts of the ice.** Put one serving of ice in one of the glass containers and put the weighted jar in the other container.

- **Fill both containers with equal amounts of water.** Using a marker or a piece of tape, mark the top of the water on each container.

- **Put the other serving of ice on a small plate placed on top of the jar.**

- **Wait until the ice melts in both containers.** Make sure that you add the water from the melted ice on the plate into the container.

- **What happened?** Which container ended up with more water? Why?

> **To investigate more,** consider that, as we've seen, one change in the world's balanced weather system affects others. In your science journal, plot out the ripple effect of rising levels of ocean waters. Don't forget that climate change affects businesses, city planning, and tourism, as well as ecosystems. Hint: Check out airports on the water's edge.

VOCAB LAB

Write down what you think each word means. What root words can you find to help you? What does the context of the word tell you?

carbon footprint, deforestation, fossil fuels, global warming, and **greenhouse gas.**

Compare your definitions with those of your friends or classmates. Did you all come up with the same meanings? Turn to the text and glossary if you need help.

GLOSSARY

abruptly: all of a sudden.

accretion: the process of growth or increase, typically by the gradual accumulation of additional layers of matter.

adaptation: a change that happens in response to the environment, often in terms of physical or behavioral characteristics that help a plant or animal survive.

air mass: a large pocket of air that has the same temperature and moisture content and differs from the air around it.

air pressure: the force of the gases surrounding the earth pressing downward, sometimes called barometric pressure.

altitude: the height of land above the level of the sea. Also called elevation.

anabatic wind: a warm wind that blows up the side of a mountain or landform.

anemometer: a device that measures wind speed.

anvil: a solid block.

Arctic air mass: a dry, cold air mass that forms over the Arctic.

arid: very dry, receiving little rain.

atmosphere: the air surrounding a planet.

atom: a small particle of matter. Atoms combine to form molecules.

aurora australis: colored lights in the sky around the South Pole. Also called the southern lights.

aurora borealis: colored lights in the sky around the North Pole. Also called the northern lights.

Automated Surface Observation System (ASOS): a system of automatic weather measurement tools.

average: a number that mathematically represents the central or middle of the measurements of something, such as temperature.

aviation: everything having to do with flight.

axis: the imaginary line through the North and South Poles that the earth rotates around.

barometer: a weather instrument that measures air pressure.

barometric pressure: the force of the atmosphere pressing downward. Also called air pressure.

BCE: put after a date, BCE stands for Before Common Era and counts down to zero. CE stands for Common Era and counts up from zero. This book was printed in 2020 CE.

Beaufort scale: a scale for measuring wind speeds, based on observation.

biodiversity: the condition in nature in which a wide variety of species live in a single area.

biomass: plant materials and animal waste used as fuel.

blizzard: a severe snowstorm with high winds, low temperatures, and heavy snow.

boundary line: the area or front between cold and warm air masses.

buoy: an anchored float that serves as a navigation or locator mark.

carbon dioxide (CO_2): a combination of carbon and oxygen that is formed by the burning of fossil fuels, the rotting of plants and animals, and the breathing out of animals or humans.

carbon footprint: the total amount of carbon dioxide and other greenhouse gases emitted over the full life cycle of a product or service or by a person or family in a year.

chaos theory: the branch of mathematics that deals with complex systems whose behavior is highly sensitive to slight changes in conditions, so that small alterations can give rise to strikingly great consequences.

circulate: to pass from place to place.

cirrus: a high-altitude cloud characterized by wispy strands.

climate: the average weather patterns in an area during a long period of time. A climatologist studies climate.

climate change: changes in the earth's climate patterns brought about by rising temperatures.

climatology: the study of climate.

cloud: a large collection of tiny droplets of water or ice crystals that are so light that they can float in the air.

coalescence: coming together and making one object out of many.

cohesive: forming a united whole.

cold front: the boundary formed by an advancing cold air mass meeting a warmer mass of air.

computer weather model: a set of numerical equations that allow computers to predict weather.

concentrated: having a lot of one substance.

condensation nuclei: very small particles in the air, such as dust or pollen, on which water vapor condenses.

condense: to change from a gas (such as water vapor) to a liquid (such as water).

conducive: making a certain situation or outcome likely or possible.

conservation: managing and protecting natural resources.

continental air mass: a vast body of air that forms over the interior of a continent.

convection cell: in meteorology, an air mass with powerful updrafts and downdrafts that can lead to severe weather.

convection: the movement of hot air rising and cold air sinking.

conveyor belt: a moving belt that carries objects from one place to another.

coral reef: an underwater ecosystem that grows in warm ocean waters and is home to millions of creatures.

core sample: a section from deep within something, such as a tree or glacier, that is taken by drilling for scientific investigation.

Coriolis effect: what happens when a mass moving in a rotating system experiences a force that's perpendicular to its motion.

correlation: a connection or relationship between two or more things.

cumulonimbus: a towering vertical cloud, generally flat-bottomed and starting at low altitudes, often signaling thunderstorms.

cumulus: a low-level, fluffy looking cloud.

current: the steady flow of water or air in one direction.

database: a collection of data, which is information in the form of facts and numbers, that can be easily searched.

deepwater current: an extremely dense, cold ocean current found at the lowest depths of oceans.

deforestation: the process through which forests are cleared to use land for other purposes.

dense: packed tightly together.

dew point: the temperature at which water vapor condenses back into liquid water.

dew: water droplets made when humid air cools at night.

disperse: to scatter over a wide area.

dissipate: to disperse, evaporate, dissolve.

Doppler radar: a type of radar used to locate precipitation, calculate its motion, and determine its type.

downdraft: a downward current of air.

downslope wind: a wind directed down a slope.

drone: an unmanned aerial vehicle.

dropsonde: a meteorological instrument dropped from an airplane.

drought: a long period of time with little or no rain.

economy: the wealth and resources of an area or country.

ecosystem: an interdependent community of living and nonliving things and their environment.

efficient: making the most of time and energy.

electromagnetic: magnetism developed with a current of electricity.

El Niño: a weather pattern that occurs when sea surface temperatures in the tropical Pacific Ocean rise to above-normal levels.

emissions: something sent or given off, such as smoke, gas, heat, or light.

equator: an imaginary line around the earth, halfway between the North and South Poles.

equilibrium: the state of balance between opposing forces.

ethanol: alcohol made from plants that can be used as fuel.

evaporate: to convert from liquid to vapor.

evolve: to change or develop slowly, during long periods of time.

exosphere: a very thin layer of gas surrounding a planet. The outer layer of Earth's atmosphere.

experiential: based on experience and observation.

eye: the calm center of the hurricane.

eye wall: powerful, spiral-shaped storms that surround the eye of a hurricane.

Ferrel cell: the global convection cell found between the Polar cell and the Hadley cell over the midlatitudes.

finite: something that is limited.

fluctuate: to change continually, shifting back and forth.

fog: a thick cloud of water droplets at or near the earth's surface.

fossil fuels: coal, oil, and natural gas. These nonrenewable energy sources come from the fossils of plants and microorganisms that lived millions of years ago.

freezing rain: rain that freezes once it lands on surfaces that are below freezing.

friction: a force that slows down objects when they rub against each other.

front: a boundary between two different air masses.

frontal cloud: a cloud that forms where the leading edge of a large moving mass of air meets another mass of air that's a different temperature.

frost: water from the air that forms tiny ice crystals on cold surfaces at night.

geostationary satellite: a satellite whose orbit follows the earth's orbit.

geothermal: heat energy from beneath the earth's surface.

glacier: a semi-permanent mass of ice that moves very, very slowly down a mountain or slope.

global ocean currents: ongoing, predictable patterns of ocean currents that flow throughout the earth's oceans. Also known as the thermohaline circulation.

global warming: an increase in the earth's average temperatures, enough to cause climate change.

global winds: ongoing, predictable patterns of winds that blow across the entire planet. Also known as prevailing winds.

gradient: an incline.

graupel: a form of freezing precipitation formed when supercooled water droplets freeze on falling snowflakes.

GLOSSARY

gravity: a force that pulls objects toward each other and all objects to the earth.

greenhouse effect: a process through which energy from the sun is trapped by a planet's atmosphere, warming the planet.

greenhouse gas: a gas in the atmosphere that traps heat. We need some greenhouse gases, but too many trap too much heat.

gyre: a large system of circulating ocean currents associated with global winds.

habitable: capable of supporting life.

habitat: the natural area where a plant or animal lives.

Hadley cell: a large-scale atmospheric convection cell in which air rises at the equator and sinks at midlatitudes.

hail: balls of ice that fall like rain.

helium: a colorless gas created in a nuclear reaction in the sun. It is the most common element in the universe after hydrogen.

high pressure: a condition of the atmosphere in which the pressure and density is above average.

hindrance: something that causes resistance, delay, or obstruction.

humidity: the amount of water vapor in the air.

hurricane: a severe tropical storm with winds greater than 74 miles per hour.

hydroelectric plant: a power plant that changes the energy from flowing water into electricity.

hydrogen: the most common element in the universe. Hydrogen and oxygen are the two elements in water.

hydrogen bond: a weak chemical bond between atoms that occurs across short distances and is easily formed and broken.

hydropower: energy produced by the movement of water.

hygrometer: an instrument that measures humidity.

ice: the solid state of water.

iceberg: a large piece of floating ice.

implication: a conclusion that can be drawn from something although it is not explicitly stated.

industrial farming: a method of large-scale farming that maximizes profit.

Industrial Revolution: a period of time during the eighteenth and nineteenth centuries when large cities and factories began to replace small towns and farming.

inextricably: in a way that is impossible to disentangle or separate.

infrastructure: the basic physical and organizational structures and facilities, such as buildings, roads, and power supplies, needed for the operation of a society or enterprise.

intermediary: a person who acts as a link between people in order to try to bring about an agreement.

intermittent: coming and going at intervals.

internal combustion engine: an engine where fuel is burned inside a cylinder.

International Space Station (ISS): a science lab in orbit about 200 miles above the earth.

interrelated: connected to one another.

Intertropical Convergence Zone (ITCZ): the area at the equator where the Northern Hemisphere's winds and the Southern Hemisphere's winds meet.

isobar: an imaginary line on a map marking places on the earth.

jet stream: a high-speed flow of air high in the atmosphere that flows from west to east and often brings weather with it.

katabatic wind: a high-speed wind that races down a mountain slope.

Köppen climate classification system: one of the most widely used climate classification systems. It divides climates into five major regions based on plant life.

land breeze: a breeze blowing from the land to the sea.

landfill: a place where waste and trash get buried between layers of soil.

landform: a physical feature of the earth's surface, such as a mountain or a valley.

latent heat: the heat that is released or absorbed when a substance changes its state.

latitude: the lines that run west and east on the globe parallel to the equator. Latitudes vary from zero degrees at the equator to 90 degrees at the North and South Poles.

lattice: a pattern of strips that are crossed with diamond-shaped spaces in between.

leeward: the side that doesn't get hit by the traveling winds.

lenticular cloud: a stationary cloud, looking like a lens or saucer, formed in the troposphere.

lightning: an electrical charge from a cloud.

local winds: sea breezes that blow onshore.

low pressure: an area in the atmosphere where the air pressure is lower than the surrounding air.

maritime air mass: an air mass formed over the ocean or sea.

mass-produce: to manufacture large amounts of a product.

mature: fully developed.

mesocyclone: a rapidly rotating air mass within a thunderstorm that often gives rise to a tornado.

mesosphere: the third layer of atmosphere away from the earth.

meteor: a rock or chunk of ice that falls toward Earth from space. Small meteors burn up before they reach Earth and we see them as shooting stars.

meteorologist: a scientist who studies weather and makes predictions about it.

meteorology: the study of weather and climate.

methane: a greenhouse gas that is colorless and odorless, composed of carbon and hydrogen.

methodical: organized.

midlatitudes: the latitude of the temperate zones found from about 30 to 60 degrees north and south of the equator.

migrate: to move from one environment to another when seasons change.

mist: tiny water droplets suspended in the atmosphere at or near the earth's surface, not as thick as fog.

mitigation: a reduction in the harmful effects of something.

molecule: a group of atoms bound together to form a new substance. Examples include carbon dioxide (CO_2), one carbon atom and two oxygen atoms, and water (H_2O), two hydrogen atoms and one oxygen atom.

National Aeronautics and Space Administration (NASA): the U.S. organization in charge of space exploration.

National Oceanic and Atmospheric Agency (NOAA): a U.S. government agency focused on the condition of the oceans and the atmosphere.

natural gas: a colorless, odorless gas that is used as fuel.

nimbus: a dark gray rain cloud.

nitrogen: the most common gas in the earth's atmosphere.

nonrenewable resource: a resource that gets used up and may not be readily replaced, such as oil.

Northern Hemisphere: the half of the earth north of the equator.

nuclear fusion: the process of hydrogen converting to helium and releasing energy and light.

occluded front: when a cold front overtakes a warm front.

offshore breeze: a breeze that originates over land.

okta: a unit of measurement used to describe the amount of cloud cover in the sky.

onshore breeze: wind that blows from water toward a landmass.

orbit: the path an object in space takes around another object.

orbital plane: the geometric plane created by the shape of an object's orbit.

organic: something that is or was living, such as wood, paper, grass, and insects.

orographic cloud: a cloud that develops because of a topographical feature, such as a mountain.

oxygen: an element that is a gas in the air. People and animals need oxygen to breathe.

ozone layer: the layer in the stratosphere that absorbs most of the sun's radiation.

paleoclimatology: the branch of science that deals with climates at particular times in the geological past.

parallel: lines extending in the same direction, keeping the same distance between them.

perpendicular: when an object forms a right angle with another object.

phenomenon: something seen or observed.

photosynthesis: the process a plant goes through to make its own food.

physicist: a scientist who studies physical forces, including matter, energy, and motion, and how these forces interact with each other.

pivotal: vitally important.

polar: the cold climate zones near the North and South Poles.

polar air mass: a cold air mass with little moisture.

polar cell: the smallest and weakest convection that extends from between 60 and 70 degrees north and south, to the poles.

polar jet: the jet stream wind circling the polar regions.

polar winds: global winds starting in the polar regions.

pollen: a fine, yellow powder produced by flowering plants. Pollen fertilizes the seeds of other plants as it gets spread around by the wind, birds, and insects.

precipitation: condensed water vapor that falls to the earth's surface in the form of rain, snow, sleet, or hail.

predetermine: to establish or decide in advance.

predictable: to know what will happen next.

predominant: for the most part, or likely.

prevailing wind: an ongoing, predictable pattern of wind that blows across the entire planet. Also known as a global wind.

prominent: important.

proxy data: data gathered about past climates by paleoclimatologists from ice cores samples, ocean sediment samples, tree rings, rocks, and fossils.

qualitative: information that is descriptive, not based on numbers.

quantitative: data that can be expressed in numbers or can be measured.

radar: a device that detects objects by bouncing radio waves off them and measuring how long it takes for the waves to return.

radiation: energy transmitted in the form of rays, waves, or particles from a source, such as the sun.

radiation fog: a low-lying cloud of water droplets that forms at night after the land cools.

radiosonde: a small, lightweight box with weather instruments and a radio transmitter.

GLOSSARY

redistribute: to alter the distribution of or give out again.

regulate: to control or adjust to keep at a certain standard.

relative humidity: the amount of water vapor present in air.

renewable energy: a form of energy that doesn't get used up, including the energy of the sun and the wind.

reservoir: a body of water that's stored for future energy use. It can be natural or man-made.

retain: to hold or keep.

ridge: a region of relatively high pressure, the opposite of a trough.

sastrugi: the irregular furrows and ridges made from wind erosion on a snowy surface. Singular is sastruga.

satellite: a spacecraft that circles the earth high above its surface to send and receive TV, cell phone, and other communications signals.

saturated: full of moisture.

sea breeze: a breeze blowing toward the land.

sea fog: a low-hanging cloud formed over the ocean.

sea level: the level of the surface of the sea.

sediment: material deposited by water, wind, or glaciers.

shock wave: a sharp change of pressure moving through the air caused by something moving faster than the speed of sound.

sleet: ice crystals that melt while they fall and then refreeze into ice pellets closer to the ground.

solar energy: energy from the sun.

solar power: energy from the sun converted to electricity.

solar system: the collection of eight planets, moons, and other celestial bodies that orbit the sun.

sophisticated: polished and smart and polite.

Southern Hemisphere: the half of the earth south of the equator.

species: a group of plants or animals that are closely related and produce offspring.

sphere: a round shape that looks like a ball.

stable air: weather that is likely to remain calm.

static electricity: an electric charge usually produced by friction between two objects.

stationary: not moving.

steam engine: an engine that burns wood or coal to heat water and create steam. The steam generates power to run the engine.

storm surge: sea water pushed along by a hurricane. It rushes inland and causes flooding when the storm reaches the coastline.

stratosphere: the layer of the earth's atmosphere above the troposphere, to about 31 miles above the earth.

stratus: a large, dark low cloud.

strife: anger or bitter disagreement.

subtle: difficult to observe.

subtropical jet: a belt of strong upper-level winds lying above regions of subtropical high pressure.

supercell: a severe thunderstorm with strong updrafts and downdrafts of air.

supercomputer: a particularly powerful mainframe computer.

supercooled: liquid cooled below its melting/freezing point without turning into a solid.

surface currents: water currents found on the surface of an ocean, driven by large-scale wind currents.

synoptic: the use of meteorological data obtained simultaneously over a wide area for the purpose of presenting a comprehensive and nearly instantaneous picture of the state of the atmosphere.

taint: to touch slightly with something bad or undesirable.

technology: the tools, methods, and systems used to solve a problem or do work.

telegraph: an electric system or device for sending messages by a code over wires.

temperate: climate or weather that is not extreme.

temperature: how warm or cold something is.

thermohaline: a type of current that moves vast amounts of water around the world.

thermometer: a weather instrument used to measure temperature.

thermosphere: the fourth layer of atmosphere above the earth.

thunderstorm: a storm with thunder and lightning that often produces heavy precipitation.

TNT: short for trinitrotoluene. A poisonous chemical mixture used as an explosive.

tornado: a violent, twisting, funnel-shaped column of air extending from a thunderstorm to the ground.

trade winds: steady winds that blow from east to west in a belt between 30 degrees latitude above the equator to 30 degrees latitude below the equator. Also called easterlies.

transpiration: the process during which plants absorb water through their roots and exhale water vapor through their leaves, stems, and flowers.

tropical cyclone: another word for hurricane.

tropical: having to do with the area around the equator.

troposphere: the lowest part of the earth's atmosphere, where most weather occurs.

trough: an elongated region of relatively low pressure, which often follows or comes in front of a high-pressure ridge.

turbine: a machine with blades turned by the force of water, air, or steam.

GLOSSARY

turbulence: violent movements in air or water.

typhoon: the name for a hurricane over the western Pacific Ocean.

ultraviolet light: a kind of light with short wavelengths. It can't be seen with the naked eye.

unstable air: air that is so warm that it continues to rise.

updraft: an upward current of air.

upslope wind: a warm wind that blows up a steep slope or mountainside.

vacuum: a space with nothing in it, not even air.

variable: a value that can change.

variation: a different form of something.

velocity: the speed of an object in a particular direction.

vulnerable: exposed to harm.

warm front: the forward boundary of a warm air mass moving to replace a retreating cold air mass.

water cycle: the continuous movement of water from the earth to the clouds and back to Earth again.

water vapor: the gas form of water.

weather: temperature, cloudiness, rainfall, and wind.

weather balloon: a helium or hydrogen balloon, equipped with meteorological devices, that is sent high into the atmosphere to provide information about weather.

weather forecast: to predict what the weather will be.

weather pattern: repeating weather during several days or weeks.

westerlies: global winds, blowing from west to east, between 30 and 60 degrees in latitude.

wind chill: what the combination of air temperature and wind feels like on your skin.

wind shear: a change in the direction of wind, especially when wind blows in different directions at different heights.

windward: the side that faces into the oncoming winds.

X-ray: a high-energy wave emitted by hot gases in the universe.

METRIC CONVERSIONS

Use this chart to find the metric equivalents to the English measurements in this activity. If you need to know a half measurement, divide by two. If you need to know twice the measurement, multiply by two.

ENGLISH	METRIC
1 inch	2.5 centimeters
1 foot	30.5 centimeters
1 yard	0.9 meter
1 mile	1.6 kilometers
1 pound	0.5 kilogram
1 teaspoon	5 milliliters
1 tablespoon	15 milliliters
1 cup	237 milliliters

RESOURCES

MUSEUMS AND PLACES TO VISIT

National Weather Museum and Science Center, Norman, Oklahoma: nationalweathermuseum.com/new-facility

National Center for Atmospheric Research (NCAR), Boulder, Colorado: ncar.ucar.edu

WEBSITES

National Aeronautics and Space Administration (NASA): nasa.gov/audience/forstudents/index.html

University Corporation for Atmospheric Research (UCAR): scied.ucar.edu/students

National Weather Service forecasts: nws.noaa.gov/forecasts.php

Scijinks: It's All About Weather by NOAA: scijinks.gov

RESOURCES

BOOKS

Carson, Mary Kay. *Weather Projects for Young Scientists: Experiment and Science Fair Ideas*. Chicago Review Press, 2007.

Davies, Nicola. *Gaia Warriors*. Candlewick Press, 2009.

Fry, Juliane L., et al. *The Encyclopedia of Weather and Climate Change: A Complete Visual Guide*. University of California Press, 2010.

Hall, Julie. *A Hot Planet Needs Cool Kids: Understanding Climate Change and What You Can Do About It*. Green Goat Books, 2007.

Woodward, John. *Weather Watcher*. DK, 2006.

SOURCE NOTES

INTRODUCTION

1 noaa.gov/weather

CHAPTER 1

1 solarsystem.nasa.gov/news/522/10-things-to-know-about-parker-solar-probe
2 esrl.noaa.gov/gmd/outreach/info_activities/pdfs/TBI_earths_atmosphere.pdf
3 Revkin, Andrew, with Lisa Mechaley. *Weather: An Illustrated History*. Sterling Publishing Co., 2018. p.45.
4 wikipedia.org/wiki/Lowest_temperature_recorded_on_Earth
5 guinnessworldrecords.com/news/2018/7/omani-town-sets-temperature-record-after-one-of-the-hottest-days-ever-monitored-531904

CHAPTER 2

1 Lynch, John. "Global Cells." *The Weather*. Firefly Books, Ltd., 2002. pp. 40–41.

CHAPTER 3

1 *The Encyclopedia of Weather and Climate Change: A Complete Visual Guide*. University of California Press, 2010. p. 87.

CHAPTER 4

1 reference.com/science/latent-heat-condensation-69ddafaffb585067
2 rainbowintl.com/blog/why-so-many-tornadoes-in-tornado-alley
3 scijinks.gov/hurricane
4 worldatlas.com/articles/hurricanes-cyclones-and-typhoons-what-is-the-difference.html

CHAPTER 5

1 earthobservatory.nasa.gov/features/WxForecasting/wx3.php
2 earthobservatory.nasa.gov/features/WxForecasting/wx3.php and nesdis.noaa.gov/content/history-noaa-satellites
3 weather.gov/media/wrn/NWS_Weather-Ready-Nation_Strategic_Plan_2019-2022.pdf

CHAPTER 6

1 *The Encyclopedia of Weather and Climate Change: A Complete Visual Guide.* University of California Press, 2010. pp. 370–371.

CHAPTER 7

1 climate.nasa.gov/faq/12/whats-the-difference-between-climate-change-and-global-warming

2 climate.nasa.gov

3 epa.gov/lmop/basic-information-about-landfill-gas and archive.epa.gov/climatechange/kids/solutions/technologies/methane.html

4 phys.org/news/2019-02-ice-free-arctic-summers-earlier-side.html

5 energy.gov/articles/top-8-things-you-didn-t-know-about-leds

6 washingtonpost.com/science/2018/12/31/extreme-weather-was-raging-howling-signal-climate-change/?noredirect=on&utm_term=.7d402a2af901

QR CODE GLOSSARY

page 5: scied.ucar.edu/dog-walking-weather-and-climate

page 7: almanac.com/content/weather-sayings-and-their-meanings

page 11: solarsystem.nasa.gov/planets/earth/overview

page 12: earthobservatory.nasa.gov/images

page 13: solarsystem.nasa.gov/solar-system/sun/overview

page 16: youtube.com/watch?v=Tu5BgjZRYKA#action=share

page 19: cimss.ssec.wisc.edu/wxfest/SunAngle/sunangle.html

page 27: science.howstuffworks.com/transport/flight/modern/question15.htm

page 29: earth.nullschool.net

page 30: youtu.be/HIyBpi7B-dE

page 32: youtube.com/watch?v=DuyyilOJrb4

page 34: wattsupwiththat.files.wordpress.com/2016/06/beaufort-wind-scale.gif

page 35: climate.ncsu.edu/images/edu/IsobarsIsotherms2.jpg

page 36: science360.gov/obj/video/4232a476-56d8-468b-bc55-bcf9427f1332/power-wind

page 37: explainthatstuff.com/anemometers.html

page 43: seametrics.com/blog/water-facts

page 44: science360.gov/obj/tkn-video/4ee06b4e-1927-42bf-8d65-267fd542270b/water-food-energy

page 46: sectionhiker.com/predicting-the-weather-using-clouds

page 47: nationalgeographic.com/science/earth/earths-atmosphere/clouds/#/1266.jpg

page 49: washingtonpost.com/news/capital-weather-gang/wp/2014/12/05/graupel-the-wintry-precipitation-youve-never-heard-of/?noredirect=on&utm_term=.93c6dc9fd63e

page 50: nationalgeographic.org/media/ocean-currents-and-climate

page 51: oceanservice.noaa.gov/facts/ninonina.html

page 53: oceanservice.noaa.gov/video/oilspill101/loop-current.html

page 54: nasa.gov/pdf/312992main_CombinedCloud2.pdf

page 54: slideplayer.com/slide/5672725/18/images/11/Cloud+Cover.jpg

page 58: youtu.be/Ym3WzJALIK0

page 61: ready.gov/tornadoes

page 64: nhc.noaa.gov/aboutsshws.php

RESOURCES

INDEX

INDEX